T0073268

ONLINE PREDATORS, AN INTERNET INSURGENCY

ONLINE PREDATORS, AN INTERNET INSURGENCY

A Field Manual for Teaching and Parenting in the Digital Arena

Second Edition

Jeffrey A. Lee

ROWMAN & LITTLEFIELD
Lanham • Boulder • New York • London

Published by Rowman & Littlefield
An imprint of The Rowman & Littlefield Publishing Group, Inc.
4501 Forbes Boulevard, Suite 200, Lanham, Maryland 20706
www.rowman.com

86-90 Paul Street, London EC2A 4NE

British Library Cataloguing in Publication Information Available

Library of Congress Cataloging-in-Publication Data

Names: Lee, Jeffrey A., 1975– author.
Title: Online predators, an internet insurgency : a field manual for teaching and parenting in the digital arena / Jeffrey A. Lee.
Description: Second edition. | Lanham : Rowman & Littlefield, [2023] | Includes bibliographical references. | Summary: "Jeffrey Lee teaches parents and stakeholders to use the tech against itself to protect children"— Provided by publisher.
Identifiers: LCCN 2023018902 (print) | LCCN 2023018903 (ebook) | ISBN 9781475870220 (cloth) | ISBN 9781475870244 (epub)
Subjects: LCSH: Internet and children—Safety measures. | Internet—Safety measures. | Online social networks—Safety measures. | Online sexual predators.
Classification: LCC HQ784.I58 L44 2023 (print) | LCC HQ784.I58 (ebook) | DDC 302.23/1083—dc23/eng/20230629
LC record available at https://lccn.loc.gov/2023018902
LC ebook record available at https://lccn.loc.gov/2023018903

For my wife, Kim, the best cheerleader, wife, mother, and friend.
For our three boys, for giving me so much joy.
It's the true honor of my life to be her husband and their father.
To my parents, Gerald and Vicki Lee, in my corner forever and always.
Online exploitation investigators are truly the best law enforcement has
to offer. To name all who've mentored or otherwise had my back would
require a book in itself. If we've worked together, I thank you.

"Children are the world's most valuable resource, and its best hope for the future."

—President John F. Kennedy

CONTENTS

FOREWORD

"There is no hunting like the hunting of man, and those who have hunted armed men long enough and liked it, never care for anything else thereafter."

–Ernest Hemingway

Online exploitation investigation is a very young discipline in the history of law enforcement—right around twenty years old. It's a very exciting-sounding opportunity many officers volunteer for . . . until they see what it actually takes to do the job. During my time as a prosecutor and division chief of a Child Exploitation Unit, I had grizzled veteran investigators coming on board ready to rock and roll. But within the first operation or two, they would tell me they were transferring out to some area that wasn't so emotionally destroying . . . like homicide.

Jeff Lee was selected to be one of the very first to join our new taskforce, coming in as a highly recommended but unknown quantity, and it was our very first operation that I saw the quality of our newest teammate. Executing a search warrant is the fun part—lots of terse exchanges, using a door ram to force entry, finding the bad guy—for that we never had any shortage of volunteers. But after the excitement of entry and securing the scene comes the paperwork-generating, tedious, but still voyeuristic search.

The real test of a new online exploitation investigator, however, comes when going through the results of the search . . . the computer forensics.

For a brand new investigator in this area, this can be a shock. It's one thing to hear about the abuses of children described in words, quite another to see the actual pictures or video.

One of the offices for the Houston Task Force was on the fourth floor of a building in the northern more affluent areas. The offices afforded an incredible view of the area, one I would often take in to clear my mind of whatever tragedy we'd dug into that day. It also gave a clear view of the parking lot below. On Jeff Lee's very first operation, we'd accomplished a successful search warrant, safely made entry, secured the scene, seized a mountain of computer evidence, and returned to the office to begin processing it all.

Myself and the other operators were curious as to what the reaction of our newest teammate would be. As the forensic preview, or computer autopsy, began, the results of child sexual abuse videos and images scrolled in report form, as they do. As the process went, taking notes and deciding which files to use for prosecution, we suddenly realized Jeff had disappeared. Maybe he'd gone to the bathroom or for coffee, so we kept working until a break was needed.

Looking out the window, we spotted Jeff walking circuits around the parking lot. This was not the first time we'd seen someone taking that walk. The real test is what happens when he's done collecting himself. After taking a few more circuits, Jeff came back up and kept going, cataloging the horrors our bad guy chose to collect. Jeff showed he had the backbone to do the job, to stand there and put his own sanity and peace of mind between the predators and the children they prey upon.

Over the years, Jeff became one of the most talented, persistent, and thorough investigators that I ever had work for me, but he's also one of the few understanding the importance of one of our other tasks. The search warrants can be exhilarating, the chase keeps you up at night, and putting the cuffs on those who abuse our children is one of the most satisfying feelings you can ever have, but being willing to teach and educate our children and their parents can actually save more lives than all of the search warrants, the manhunts, and incarceration time put together. Jeff is one of the investigators who threw himself into not just hunting the bad guys but arming our children and parents with the knowledge to protect themselves. Jeff works endlessly at schools and parenting events to provide the armor to keep themselves safe. It's our hope his book, *Online Predators, an Internet Insurgency*, will go even further in the endless battle for our children.

In this second edition of the book, Jeff delves into some of the changing landscapes of the fight against child exploitation, but also to the mental health concerns of exposure to child exploitative crimes, both from a victimization and investigative standpoint. The images and videos these crusaders are exposed to burn into the very depths of their brains, and many fall victim to the mental health impact this work inflicts. It is significant and lasting on the warriors who volunteer to protect our children. I know this because it had a lasting impact on my own mental health. It's been over ten years since I worked child exploitation cases full-time, and it took a good chunk of those years for the images and videos to not visit me every time I closed my eyes at night. Please do not mistake my meaning, the child exploitation assignment was the most fulfilling of my career, but the costs were massive.

I want to thank Jeff for providing this resource to parents and stakeholders in this fight. While teaching internet safety to parents, this is my favorite resource to pass out to parents needing a deeper look than an hour-long speaking engagement will give them.

So, from the brothers and sisters of the task forces who spend the days and nights, weekdays and weekends, and regular days and holidays fighting the evil of those who prey on our children, we hope this book gives you the armor needed to protect your children and join us in our fight to protect others. I'm not sure if it takes a village to raise a child, but in today's cyberworld, it takes one to protect them.

Eric Devlin, JD, BA; investigator, digital forensics expert, and
former child exploitation chief prosecutor and task force co-commander

PREFACE

When it comes to the safety and security of children, there's no trump card to that deck. Many of the dangers they face are beyond the scrutiny of those charged with their protection and education. Physical, sexual, or emotional abuse may take place behind closed doors with victims sworn to secrecy or else facing unspeakable consequences from their abusers.

But even in the most stable of households teamed with trusted, dedicated educational and school support systems, there's a form of emotional and sexual abuse rarely manifesting itself until it explodes beyond the child's intellectual capabilities.

There's no way to gently introduce the topic of online child exploitation. Readers of this book are going to be sickened, scared, and angry at times, sometimes a very jarring mixture of all three. What's covered in this book is a small percentage of actual online depravity. Full exposure to this underworld isn't necessary to spur action in the fight to keep children safe.

My goal with this glimpse is that the reader will be *compelled* to do anything they can in order to protect the children in their charge.

Also, this book is *not* a comprehensive guide for all things that can happen in the world of online child exploitation and its prevention. Covering this topic fully would require many more volumes, as exploitation techniques change almost daily with the technology. This book is meant to support and encourage stakeholders to develop a curiosity about their children's online lives and immerse themselves in it.

There's a 1988 movie called *They Live*. This science fiction follows an average man who finds sunglasses allowing him to see things invisible to ordinary people. He sees aliens living on Earth, disguised as people, and machinery in place to beam mind-controlling media to keep their existence a secret.

If a pair of sunglasses could somehow illuminate everyone with an incurable, consuming, unchangeable sexual preference for children, they would be seen at ball games, pediatrician offices, schools, churches, convenience stores, post offices, driving school buses, piloting jet liners, sitting in a car at the traffic light, in line at the grocery store, in a police uniform, firefighter's bunker gear—basically anywhere children gather or anyone they are drawn to.

And if a light were shown over every house containing child sexual abuse imagery, there would be no commute home or to work without seeing several.

An article in the *New York Times*[1] highlights the issue in mainstream media, which doesn't happen very often, perhaps due to the fact that "few people want to confront the enormity and horror of the content, or they wrongly dismiss it as primarily teenagers sending inappropriate selfies."

Irresponsible teenagers sending their nude images back and forth is a large part of the problem, as these images very often end up with unintended recipients. But this is a head-in-the-sand attitude when confronted with the term *preferential sex offender*. This means they prefer certain traits in their victims, which include but are not limited to height, weight, hair color, eye color, musculature, gender, and *age*. Combine that with the Merriam Webster's definition of pornography: "The depiction of erotic behavior (as in pictures or writing) intended to cause sexual excitement."

Nearly everyone has seen some form of pornography at some point in their lives—human beings engaged in all manner of sexual activity. It's segregated into innumerable genres—bondage, foot fetish, sado-masochistic, homo- and heterosexual, bestiality, to name a few. So if there are millions of people whose sexual objects are children and suspects seek what they're aroused by, this is *what's driving the child pornography marketplace*.

Child pornography has always been used as a powerful grooming tool with children. It is used to normalize sexual contact between adults and children, and to get them to produce pornography of their own.

Child pornography follows technology: eight-millimeter film to VHS to digital files, darkroom developed photos to digital files, underground print magazines to dark websites. What was once the exclusive hunting ground of the US Postal Service (illegal mailing of videos, film, magazines) is now open season for the largest to the smallest law enforcement agencies worldwide. Law enforcement cannot arrest its way out of this issue. There are simply too many predators.

The prevalence and permanence of social media, electronic devices, and the Information Autobahn are an integral part of children's lives: They don't know life without it. To parents and educators of this current generation, there's a frame of reference their children don't have—life before this personal technology. A generation of parents who got their first email address in their twenties is raising a generation teething on the corners of an iPad.

Merriam-Webster defines "friend" as one attached to another by affection or esteem. It's further emphasized as someone a person knows to hug, cry with, celebrate with, in other words, *in the physical company of one another*. Today, physical company includes a Facetime call. One no longer has to breathe the same air as another to develop said affection and esteem. In essence, a child physically alone in their room, as their parents were at their age, is often times not alone.

There's a lot of emphasis on the technology itself—the apps, the dizzying array of a modern smartphone screen—leading some to the conclusion they're impossible to keep up with and that's completely understandable. But this technology holds the key to both protecting children and securing their futures tied to it. As General Stanley McChrystal says in his book *Team of Teams*, "Interconnectedness and the ability to transmit information instantly can endow small groups with unprecedented influence: the garage band, the dorm room startup, the viral blogger, and the terrorist cell."[2]

General McChrystal's topic for that book was the fundamental management changes his Special Operations group needed in order to fight a determined and ruthless enemy, the Iraqi Insurgency following the United States invasion.. The same is to be said of this fight against online child exploitation, and I'll equate online predators with the modern terrorist cells, whether they're white supremist or jihadist: individual child predators forming interconnected groups with shared goals (the online exploitation of children) becoming exponentially more powerful as a whole rather than the one thanks to technology.

Child predators, whether they are perverts or sex traffickers, are an insurgency as defined by Merriam Webster: the quality or state of being insurgent, specifically a condition of revolt against a government that is less than an organized revolution and that is not recognized as a belligerency. Predators are revolting against a very personal government, our parental authority. They are not organized as they aren't pronounced. They sneak in and strike with no warning, inflicting serious damage in our lives. Child predators are well beyond the stubborn, insistent, and belligerent spam emails or pop-up ads. They represent a clear and present danger to the safety and security of a child and to a stakeholder's abilities to keep that child safe and under their control.

General McChrystal came to the conclusion that traditional, proven techniques of the past were no longer adequate and were, in some cases, obsolete.

No longer can we simply just keep constant eyes on our children while shopping, tell them to stay away from white vans driven by strangers offering candy, bar the doors and windows, and remote-lock school doors to keep our children safe. We now face dangers beamed inside our own houses by WiFi, and we must adapt accordingly. To fight this insurgency, you'll need to join the more than 670,000 local, state, and national law enforcement professionals because we're outnumbered by these insurgents.

This is a call to all parents, guardians, extended family, and educators, the stakeholders in the lives of children. Together, we'll far outnumber child predators. After ten years of fighting online child exploitation, I've concluded this war cannot be won without the active involvement of stakeholders. The frontlines aren't just for law enforcement.

It's in your homes and schools, little league fields, ballet and gym classes, Sunday schools, PTA groups—wherever stakeholders and children intersect.

This book is written to propose a simple yet fundamental change to parenting and educating styles, one that's immune to the lightspeed pace of technology. The only way to win this fight is to radically reduce, and ideally eliminate, the pool of potential victims of online predation.

Stakeholders have to physically inspect their children's devices. They must establish open and clear communication about online predation and present expectations about device usage and consequences for not adhering to them. And if the educational systems are making use of this technology mandatory and put school-issued technology in their hands, there must be curriculum and enforcement of digital citizenship and crime prevention in the classroom as regular as fire drills.

We have to take care of the already known victims of online child exploitation, these casualties of this war. Additionally, we have to locate, identify, and treat those victims still unknown and out there. Physical injuries can heal to the point that there's no evidence the injury ever happened. The mental health damage to not only victims but also to those who love, teach, and protect them is a much harder problem to quantify and treat but just as important as bruises and broken bones.

The views and opinions in this book are solely mine and are the result of more than twenty years of law enforcement training and experience, the majority of it spent fighting online child exploitation. Although these ideas I put forth do not represent those of any law enforcement entity or organization, they are universally agreed upon as some of the best practices of prevention. The shame of it is the opportunities missed time and again by stakeholders to detect online predation before it becomes an immovable force in a child's life.

Many factors cause untold damage: from parents and educators focused on respecting children's "right to privacy" by not monitoring the contents of their devices, to ignoring furtive and secretive behavior, not making online predation a topic of regular family conversations and lesson plans, overlooking online associations between teacher and students, the misapplication of a child's online access as a right and not a product of pre-established trust, and just plain unfettered, uncontrolled, irresponsible allowance of the child's access to the whole world and that world's access to the child.

The bottom line is that a person who places tech in the hands of a child bears the responsibility to teach that child digital citizenship and safety. If one purchases a cell phone for the child with the main goal of antagonizing their ex-spouse, that parent has made both themselves and the reluctant ex accountable for guiding the child in cyberspace. This is not to confuse responsibility for online predation. That sits squarely on the shoulders of the predator who broke their bond with society to protect and nurture young people.

This book is to empower and encourage stakeholders (parents, guardians, relatives, and educators, basically any adult with an interest, concern, and investment in a particular child's life) to take a proactive rather than reactive approach to a child's online life.

NOTES

1. Keller, Michael H., and Gabriel Dance. "The Internet is Overrun with Images of Child Sexual Abuse. What Went Wrong?" *New York Times*, September 28, 2019. https://www.nytimes.com/interactive/2019/09/28/us/child-sex-abuse.html.

2. McChrystal, Stanley. *Team of Teams.* New York: Penguin Random House, 2015.

INTRODUCTION

Best-selling author David Morrell's most famous character is John Rambo. His several other writings and screenplays put millions of words under his pen. One of these books, *Lessons Learned from a Lifetime of Writing*, is part memoir and part instructional manual for aspiring writers. In this book, Morrell asks a very important question: Why does one want to become a writer?

His answer is an extremely personal one. A writer wants to be a writer because they simply *have* to. There's simply something inside a person that just has to get out. So before writing this second edition, this author broadened the question into why did this author *have* to write the first edition of *Online Predators, An Internet Insurgency*? The first thought was: nobody else could write this exact book because this author's observations, experiences, and conclusions are his and his alone, and something inside him insisted the book be written.

The reason this author chose to write this second edition is because he owes it to his victims to perfect this work and do all he can do to protect children and families from the dangers of online exploitation. Since 2020, when the first edition of this book was published, technology has continued its unstoppable march forward, leading to dangerous new elements to the predator threat stream.

In 2008, the Blackberry was still the King of Phones, and the iPhone just debuted with two gigabytes of available internal storage. The social media tsunami was just beginning to roll. The US Congress passed the Protect

Our Children Act, which required the development of a National Strategy for Child Exploitation Prevention and Interdiction, an organized, concerted effort to detect, thwart, and prosecute online exploiters of children.

The research done to support the act recognized the evolution of investigators from service to the local citizenry to serving people all over the country, and as it turned out, the whole world. The common bonds of the internet and technology have continued to shrink the planet, just as the telegraph, telephone, and television did years ago.

In the schools, SmartBoards replaced blackboards, laptops, and tablets favored over traditional pen and paper notetaking. Apps like Google Classroom have revolutionized the homework business. Teachers communicate directly with parents via email and even Zoom. These advances require connection to the internet, and with it, a device to do so. A parent's decision to equip their child with a smartphone is being made by necessity, rather than the child being ready to accept and understand the implications and responsibility that goes along with it.

It's mostly a positive thing, this making electronic devices a "job" requirement for children, but it can also be hugely negative as criminal online predators also go cyber. This is the easiest way yet to access children. So with this "job" requirement, it brings together parents and educators in the fight to protect children in this true Information Age, whose commodity of images and text is a weapon as potent as any assault rifle or bunker-busting bomb. As the human race has come to need, to crave, this information inundation, it results in phones checked first thing in the morning. Information has surpassed the need for coffee.

As a kid on road trips back in the day, after burning through the books, games, and other distractions parents picked up to keep their children quiet and occupied, invariably the children would start in on each other.

The dad, without fail, would get their attention, looking at them through the rearview mirror, over the top of his glasses, and say something like "Fold your hand and watch the traffic."

Not exactly a cure for boredom, but there was a limit on what he could suggest on day two of a three-day road trip to visit the grandparents. Today, it would have to be one heck of a long trip to bore kids to the point of picking on siblings. Between the phones and tablets, there's enough distraction to keep them occupied as the world zips by.

Technology has made it an exciting and challenging time to be an educator. With virtual reality three-dimensional experiences to study ancient monuments and sculptures, interactive classrooms from the International Space Station and Antarctica, to real-time homework help, a teacher has the capability to reach and impact students not only in their classroom, but all across the world.

This unprecedented interaction between students and educators brings a Tesla coil of creativity and a level of excitement in the classroom that chalkboards, physical textbooks, and DVDs couldn't. But the personal lives of students and teachers on display via social media give access to each other's lives outside the classroom. Becoming too familiar with one another, even if it begins nobly as a way to research, can lead to passive online stalking.

On the flipside of that coin, in this share-everything-on-social-media atmosphere, children throw out all kinds of indicators they're in some kind of trouble. What happens then? It's not safe to assume the child's parents are aware of it. They may not even be aware that the child's social media accounts exist.

The real impetus for writing this book came when a toddler family member, barely walking and talking, somehow picked up an iPad and managed to FaceTime another family member. There she was, drool and all, laughing and smiling, even playing peek-a-boo. She is part of the first fully digitally integrated generation in the history of the world.

Unmonitored communication between children and felony sex criminals is the scourge of the Information Age. Technology and its devices (hardware, software, games, etc.) can be a life-altering hairpin turn of kids' lives. In addition, this book will show how all stakeholders in a child's life can detect, or even better, avert, the consequences of online predation. Parents, guardians, grandparents, aunts, uncles, educators, and even siblings are the platoon of defense.

This book is going to inform, educate, and empower anyone to protect loved ones and those in their charge from the negative effects of many types of cyber-crime. It will acquaint the reader with the best practices to analyze situations and provide ground rules to teach children how to keep themselves safe online. Because if children are not empowered as well, the fight is even tougher.

Part of the work will be to establish appropriate behavior with children before the tech is in their hands. And if schools are going to require the use of devices and applications to successfully complete academic requirements, there's a heavy burden on educators to reinforce internet safety in the classroom. For those parenting and educating teens and tweens using devices already, the job is to rewrite the rules governing device use and rein in reckless usage. Both are accomplished in ways similar to how kids are taught to behave in a restaurant or a classroom. Expectations are laid out along with consequences for not adhering to them.

Does this guarantee a nice night out at the dinner table or a utopian classroom setting? Absolutely not, as any parent or teacher can attest. But food fights, nose picking, staring and flinching contests over dinner, talking out of turn, going to the bathroom without a pass, and disrespect in a classroom are guaranteed if the rules aren't laid out. As stakeholders in children's lives, a disaster of one type or another seems just one step away at times. It's just the nature of the business.

Here's the needed anchor. It is vitally important to protect children from cyber-crime, cyber-bullying, and the damage to their futures the laws of unintended consequences inflict. It is important to risk and experience the temper tantrums, name-calling, eye rolling, and dramatic sighs in the overall accomplishment of keeping the child safe.

The discussion in the following chapters is going to revolve around three simple but important questions:

- Are stakeholders aware of what children face online?
- Is it too hard or outside of a stakeholder's business to deal with?
- Is there a good plan to deal with what's discovered?

Reaching out for information on tech and children is a step in the right direction. Safely parenting and educating the tech-minded youth is all about stakeholder involvement for proactive prevention and early detection, rather than reactive damage control.

All this being said, the very idea of a written book about guiding youth in Internet-land is a daunting one. Do not construe the following pages as rigid rules, but rather a fluid framework, like a snake making its way around things in the way, because that's what guiding children is like in real life, right? Every child is different, with innumerable needs, wants, and past experiences. When coupled with the stakeholders' own life experiences, requirements, and station in life, along with the ever-evolving nebula of technology, the actions become extremely complex.

Many stakeholders just want the recipe for safe online children handed to them like a program at the beginning of a concert or school play. But there's just too many complicated variables involved for that to be possible. As online exploitation investigators attest, these crimes against children do follow common patterns, but *no two cases are ever exactly alike*. Each day brings an investigator, child, and stakeholder to a place they've never been before.

So it stands to reason there's no absolute "right" way to approach and deal with online predation in the home, school, or other child-centric environment. Stakeholders are in a much better position armed with a focused curiosity of their tech-minded children, fueled by the concepts in this book, and with solid methods of deterrence, detection, and mitigation.

Most books on internet safety for children focus on the technology, which is a natural and worthwhile cornerstone considering the problem at hand. However, this book takes a different approach, because what good is an internet safety guide revolving around technology as it was in 2008, 2010, or 2012 when it is 2020 or 2050 when it is read? These books can and do remain for sale well after the problem tech of their day has been pushed aside.

The hope for this book is that the reader will see past all the glitter and tech glitz for the in-between: the problem of online predation can be attacked with the age old parenting proverb: *who, what, where, why, and how?* Who is the child hanging out with? What are they doing? Where are they doing it? Why is it happening? How is it happening?

In chapters 1 and 2, the freedoms of the internet allow for unmitigated flow of the internet's most dangerous commodity: information. It's the currency of device usage, and the exchange rate is often lopsided when it's applied to relationships and people's motivations.

A common theme throughout those chapters is the permanency of artifacts that information creates which can and should be used to detect and deter online predation. These artifacts are further explored in chapter 3 as the ins and outs of the Fourth Amendment are applied in the home and school environments.

Chapters 4 and 5 contend with the components of truth. Role-playing games such as the *Call of Duty* franchise have revolutionized the way armed services approach recruitment. There's very little difference between a commercial for a role-playing game warfare game and a military enlistment ad these days. There's little need to gloss over the military existing to kill a nation's enemies because children and young adults are already exposed to it. The sheer numbers of available victims online have allowed predators to be more truthful too, and they use "Creeper Messages" to reach out.

In the not-so-distant past, the decision on when to equip a child with a device(s) was more of one about the child being ready emotionally and responsibility wise. Chapter 6 discusses how devices have become indispensable in people's lives. Chapter 7 begins the discussion on how the data a phone is programmed to keep can be used to understand how it's being used. The stakeholder will learn more about using the technology against itself to monitor a child's device usage by reviewing data the device automatically keeps.

Chapters 8 and 9 deal with how child predators seek out their victims and how the emotional immaturity of device users are exploited by predators. These chapters explain the lengths predators will go to not only gain the trust and favor of the child, but the use of gifted devices to the child to enable them to produce the imagery discussed in the other chapters. Chapters 10 and 11 continue to explore the permanency of device artifacts by discussing photographs, the sheer amount of dangerous information unwittingly released by the careless use of these pictures, and the types of sexual abuse imagery and how they are used by predators.

Chapters 12 and 13 illustrate how predators and even scam artists will exploit the types of pictures discussed in the previous two chapters. These romance and hookup scams are a new and evolving threat to children and extremely common as they are effective to induce the production of sexually explicit imagery by victims. Then, these scammers attempt to extort money from their victims.

For chapters 14, 15, and 16, the discussion begins on developing plans for introducing children to technology, from what type of device to buy all the way to what to expect from law enforcement should the need arise. Enforcing the proactive rather than reactive model, it is time to formulate plans for device monitoring and examination, cover salient talking points with children and students, and discuss home/school safety issues in the event child predation is discovered. At this point, it will be plainly evident why all the information kept about a child's devices and online accounts comes together as the first positive mitigation step when law enforcement must become involved.

Chapter 17 provides information on what to expect after a police report and investigation are conducted, emphasizing the need for follow up self-care and therapy. Chapter 18 is a continuing discussion on real-life versus online interactions, further reinforcing the differences between online and real life and why it is of utmost importance children are imbued with the differences between the two. All users of social media, not just children, spend large amounts of time crafting posts, responses, and text messages to convey just the right, desired message and response. Child predators do this just as well, and with devastating results.

Chapters 19 and 20 provide guidance on discussing the real-life implications of not adhering to the safety standards the stakeholder sets, including a case study of just how serious these consequences can get. Just as dangerous as the predators are those involved in human trafficking. Traffickers are using these same social media tactics to lure children to leave safe environments on their own volition, not by force.

The daily lives of online child exploitation investigators can be examined to see just how busy they are due to the pervasiveness of technological crimes. There are lessons for everyone in how they cope with their jobs, as will be seen in chapters 21 and 22.

This second edition will cover new and emerging threats like miniature GPS tracking devices and case studies to support these new trends. Also new is a focus on mental health and aftercare for victims, families, and investigators. This book will continue to hammer home the importance of a clean online reputation in a young adult's life because the good news is that it's not all bad. From this point forward, all children will grow into adulthood with social media and devices as staples, not curious inventions plopped down midlife. Their world is forever tied to the internet, producing opportunities not possible before. Social media will be their business card, cyberspace their marketplace, and their devices the conduit to it all. The goal is to get them there, ready both emotionally and physically, to utilize it to their fullest potential. Nothing turns the light on fear like confidence in knowledge. Thank you for picking up this book and sharing time with this author, whose goal is to not waste a second of it.

TO SHARE OR NOT TO SHARE ISN'T THE QUESTION

Merriam-Webster defines "share" as the act of dividing a portion of something with another or others. To partake of, use, experience, occupy, or enjoy with others. They've even included a definition to apply it to social media as to tell others one's thoughts, feelings, or experiences with others.

The word share is catchy, and since sharing is taught at a young age, it's the polite thing to do, right? So complete strangers are let in on thoughts and feelings, pictures and videos that not long ago would only be shared with someone a person actually knows *personally*. If a tree falls in the forest and no one is around to hear it, does it make a sound? Likewise, if there's a thought expressed online and doesn't get enough likes, it is devalued to the point of deletion.

Silence is a vacuum social media abhors. And contributions are often not any better than silence. Imagine if one day all the social media apps, instead of text comments, switched to voice memos. Opening the typical Twitter or Instagram feed would find thousands of conversations and comments going on, all at once. Every single word colliding and clinking, crashing like a tray of fine china, or worse, a whole school having lunch in the cafeteria *at the same time.* But that's what social media is—a million conversations passing in front of your eyes, translated by brains, bouncing around in skulls.

What might happen if one didn't share everything? Human beings are explorers, chasers, challengers. It's what pushes people to become teachers, astronauts, scientists, and researchers. These characteristics also are what attracts people to one another, the mystery and enigma of someone new, the "Hold the presses, who is that?" rush of excitement.

Rather than engage directly with that person to get the answers, there's a passive, nearly risk-free way to figure all that stuff out, and that's social media. A whole life is there. Likes, dislikes, their idea of a perfect soulmate in that personality quiz taken a month ago and forgotten, what they do on the weekends, and, lest it be left out, what they had to eat in the last month.

It's easy to see how people can come to see others for someone in inappropriate circumstances, like a teacher and a student. Absent social media, there's very little chance of an educator seeing a female student poolside in a bikini or a male student shirtless washing their pickup truck. And as they invariably do, students' insecurities manifest themselves in comments and taglines, making it easier to exploit these weaknesses *by an educator who already has a sexual interest in children.* Sadly, it's very common for investigators to find a longstanding sexual fixation on children by educator/predators long before they ever set foot in a classroom. As will be set forth in this book, educator/predators are the ultimate definition of child predators.

They put themselves intentionally into positions affording easy access to children.

Besides teacher/educator, other types of predatory relationships thrive in this environment. So when it comes to a child's social media, all the snippets of insecurities either in written form or the slightly risqué bikini mirror pictures, the personality quizzes buried in a newsfeed full of backstory are neon lights of attraction to those who mean them harm. Gone are the days of gaining a potential victim and family's trust, of observing and exploiting the cracks in a kid's life, or the intense grooming it took to get close enough to a kid to sexually exploit them.

Those decisions are now made by predators after careful consideration of information on social media. These suspects are more likely to go after a sure thing, in much the same way a car burglar bypasses one car for another merely because it's unlocked. Social media has made people lazy in terms of information gathering, and luckily, it is making the perverts lazy too. Controlling available information can make the child a harder target, one that might be skipped in favor of something more accessible.

When somebody mentions the police, perhaps most often the thought is the visible patrol car, making the rounds deterring criminal activity. Most of the nighttime activities of citizens, such as locking doors and windows at night, beeping the car alarm, all in an effort to feel safe, are a hedge against what law enforcement invariably misses. Police cannot be in the right places at the right times all that often, as the Uniform Crime Reports and blasts on Nextdoor and Facebook attest.

The public expects law enforcement to deal with human garbage, but, by and large, they don't want to know anything about how it's done. To know would be to know just how close the wildness is to the gates.

Veteran internet crimes against children investigators see hundreds, if not thousands, of child victims filmed doing things no child should ever comprehend. These are literally crime scene photos and videos, taken so that some volunteer baseball coach, teacher, boy or girl scout leader, priest, or pediatrician with a secret sexual interest in children can collect and view. Sadly, that same child brought by their parents to say hello in a fast-food joint often reminds these investigators of a victim they've seen in their work. It's a common symptom of post-traumatic stress disorder in these investigators.

A couple of times a month, if not more, all over the country, there's a small circle of patrol personnel and investigators giving a briefing at zero dark thirty. This heavily armed team is going over the operations plan targeting a local mobile home park or even a thirty-thousand-square-foot mansion. Child pornography lives in the evil hearts of human beings, whether they are a chief executive officer or a person experiencing homelessness. The only difference is the amount of area to search.

1

INFORMATION AS A WEAPONIZED COMMODITY

Information is the most powerful weapon wrought against kids. It's become like water and air—both are abundant elements in daily life. Information is mostly free, portable, and potent. Too much given out, too much coming in. A word often used during these pandemic times is misinformation. This can be defined as "false or inaccurate information, especially that which is deliberately intended to deceive." This is what used to be called a lie, a fabrication, or a falsehood. The reality is information is either true or false. On or off, another binary commodity. Often trust (whether of strangers or so-called friends) is freely given by kids and not earned, as it should be. Trust is like gasoline and oil. The more there is of anything, the cheaper it gets. Educators are first-hand witnesses to the volatility of friendships in elementary, middle, and high school. Amigos one day, not the next; text messages between ex-BFFs get screenshotted and passed around. Human beings were created as forgetful, that's why these devices exist to begin with, but they create permanent artifacts. An argument in person, voice to voice and face to face, fades with memory as to who said what and how it was said.

Eventually, anger diminishes along with the memories and amends can be made. But in a text argument, the hurts are revisited, reabsorbed, and what may have been a lifelong friendship renewed may never be again. All because of the permanency of the artifacts.

But as stakeholders in the guidance and education of children, what's needed is understanding the oversharing, permanency, and pervasiveness of the devices can be used to gain an advantage. In pre-digital times, a daughter may have kept a diary of her thoughts and troubles hidden in her room. Any curiosities about sex, relationships, and typical teenage concerns would have appeared as *Cosmopolitan* magazines secretly obtained and kept, as she learned what guys are attracted to or ways to ensure a guy called back after a first date. Educators would intercept handwritten notes passed around classrooms or recovered after being dropped in the hallways, or would listen in the halls as they monitored between-class traffic. Obviously, those days are long gone.

One might think a handwritten note would be the ultimate permanent artifact, but that's thinking in the tangible sense of a more traditional definition of the word artifact. Often, a piece of pottery or arrowheads from an ancient culture in a museum is what is thought of when the term artifact comes to mind. The problem with physical, tangible artifacts like pottery and the handwritten note is simple—it requires a physical place to be stored, like a museum or a shoebox shoved back on the top shelf of a closet. The smaller the space available and the ease of storage results in a trade-off with its importance. Less-important items can be decided to be kept or discarded due to how easy it is to store them. The biggest example of this is perhaps the fact that nearly all the readers of this book can recall receiving and even cherishing handwritten gossip notes received or discovered back in the day. But how many actually still have them now, as adults, twenty or more years after they were written?

If a stakeholder really wants to check the barometer of their kid's mental status, concerns, and overall condition, the devices are the new diaries.

Want to know if they have health issues they're afraid to talk about? Dr. Google is where everybody turns, and so do they. A common type of case reported to online crimes against children investigators is that a parent discovered their daughter was receiving gifts from an unknown online male friend because very risqué lingerie was found hidden in her closet. Often, the result of that investigation reveals the child ordered them for herself after converting babysitting cash to gift cards, and since she beat her parents home by three hours every day, it was easy to intercept the packages off the porch. If this mother had just taken up the daughter's device, the answer was right there.

Educational institutions set rigorous rules in place in regards to device usage during school hours to eliminate distractions caused by their usage. Without them, a classroom of twenty-five to forty students would be a nasty symphony of vibrations, dings, and song ringtones. Children would be running into each other in the halls between classes, their heads downward at their screens. Consequences for breaking usage rules, such as confiscation, detention, suspension, and monetary bounties for return of confiscated devices, weigh heavily on the students and dissuade usage.

That being said, device usage in the face of these consequences is a big red flag of something large and important, or even distressing in that student's life. As will be explored in a case study later in this book, an educator seeing beyond the disciplinary problem for what it was saved that child from an in-person predatory encounter, and quite possibly, from death.

All the burning questions stakeholders had in years past, their worries and concerns, are the very same ones faced today. How many times did stakeholders of previous generations wish there was a one-stop solution to finding out what's up with their kids? Now it's available in their devices. Stakeholders buy the devices, pay for the service, and give them to the children. So why not pick them up and inspect them? This is one big way the digital problems need to be fought: by using the tech itself.

Here are some parent-specific questions to ask and then write down the answers:

- How many devices does each child in the household have?
- What about "sub-devices"? These are smartphone applications for texting and calling that allow that phone to have another, different phone number.
- What email accounts do the children have, and what are the passwords?
- What are the kids' usernames/gamer tags? Does the stakeholder know what a gamer tag is?
- What are their passwords and PIN codes?
- What social media accounts do the kids have? What are the usernames/passwords for those?
- Are stakeholders friends/following/followers of their children's accounts so they see what they post?
- Learn about separate, fake, or "throw down" accounts used for clandestine communications. An example would be a "Finsta," or a fake Instagram, most often used to publish risqué photographs not ordinarily shared on a profile a stakeholder knows about.

For educators, it's important to be aware of how much power to protect children from online dangers is in their possession. By virtue of how much time is spent with them, whether in front of a classroom or during one-on-one instruction, there are ripe opportunities for detection and intervention.

And terse email exchanges about classroom matters notwithstanding, parents/guardians depend on every stakeholder in their children's lives to help protect them. Here's some questions and concerns for educators:

- Students seen managing more than one cell phone at a time is suspect. Often, children use one device as a "public," or parent-sanctioned device, and another for secretive usage.
- A student risking their precious digital freedom by using a device during prohibited times at school is motivated by something important. Often, it's a clandestine online predatory relationship. Try to find ways to go beyond the disciplinary issue toward the root cause of the behavior.
- Are there ways to bring up internet safety in everyday lesson plans?
- Ideas for internet safety lessons can be found online, such as the National Center for Missing and Exploited Children and NetSmartz (netsmartz.org).

Information is the currency of device usage, but all too often the exchange rate is wildly uneven and, unfortunately, sold too cheap. Exploiters of other humans always have trust from someone they did not earn, to exclude their victims. A spouse, significant other, siblings, an employer perhaps. This is possible because there are two distinct sides of someone—the predatory life is kept separate from the other. It is much like a computer that's been set up to run multiple operating systems on the same machine. Most often it's just two operating systems that would ordinarily compete with one another: Mac and Windows, Windows and Linux. Instead of competing, they exist on the same computer, pull from the same data sources, and can be actively switched back and forth from one another in the same session. This is the same with predators and exploiters—the father and abuser, the coach and abuser, and so on.

Stakeholders, however, can use the permanency of that information to cash in on the big payoff of exploitation detection. It's a matter of placing themselves in a position to get it.

To Recap:

- Technology creates permanent artifacts which can be examined for important information.
- Devices are a one-stop barometer of children's lives and conditions.
- Make, and periodically update, lists of devices, accounts, passwords, etc.

2

FREEDOMS OF THE INTERNET

There's a lot of talk about freedom of the internet—digital rights and the free flow of information and ideas. At its core, the internet is a utility. Electric companies bill for kilowatts and water companies for gallons used, and the internet in gigabytes and the speed of service. Beyond that, the internet's true value is in living units of creativity, making the internet a living, evolving embodiment of human potential. It can be the best and, unfortunately, the worst people are capable of.

When dealing with the worst that people are capable of online, most of the time it's a byproduct of the perception of anonymity in an online environment. Some people believe no one knows who they are and that they can't ever be found out. In essence, they are free to do whatever they want. Consider the threat of an active shooter on a school campus. A student decides to use an "anonymous" app on her phone to send a message that she is the shooter and is on campus. It is a geo-based application. This means that only users in the immediate area will see this message. So, a student with the app sees that threatening message and tells another student, and so on and so forth, until frightened parents begin showing up at the school to take their kids home. This results in a total disruption of the school day, and even accidents on the roadways as concerned parents rush to the school.

The actual investigative steps in this kind of case will not be discussed, but in the end, law enforcement tracks the suspect student down, and when interviewed, she says she felt "safe" in posting the threat because she used an application billing itself as anonymous. She did it because she didn't want to take a math test that day. The way most people use the internet, nothing online is anonymous. These machines and networks can't operate out of thin air. Commands and interactions require artifacts, which are the inputs of the user. The threatening statement "I am the shooter" is the artifact. In order to broadcast her statement as the app is designed to do, it had to create timestamps and collect information on the post to make it all go.

A truly anonymous application doesn't exist because without users' data, there is no money to be made. Every user input can be monetized. Phone numbers, email addresses, login information . . . all of it can be sold to other entities. And if the service is free, like Twitter, Facebook, and Instagram, the money has to be made somewhere, and that money is made with the users' data.

Even the word "data" is extremely impersonal. A person's "data" is a sanitized way of saying one's habits, secret attractions, obsessions, crushes, wishes, thoughts, hatreds, fetishes, desires, wants, needs, biases, prejudices, political beliefs, religious leanings, sexual orientation, clothing preferences, lingerie choices, sexual habits, medical concerns, fears, hopes, flirtations, unresolved conflicts, psychological conditions, projections, financial situations, shopping patterns, menstrual cycles, food preferences, and so on, all the way up to one's natural hair color and beyond. And it's all fed into a series of giant mathematical equations called algorithms. In order to be part of the online world, a user must be reduced and converted to computer code—stripped of flesh, blood, and emotion. A user's humanity means nothing in this world, and the dissociation is lost on the user.

A writer may choose to make a first draft entirely in longhand, with a pen and paper, thus creating a physical artifact. A written manuscript conveys the circumstances in which it was written. A reader can tell if the writer was in a hurry, or a pause for thought can be indicated by unequal spacing. A trained linguist could even tell if the writer quit mid-thought and came back to the manuscript later. This is somewhat true with word processing on a computer, but one has to go looking for it by turning on the review functions.

Any time one operates in a theater devoid of any emotive quality, it's in this disconnect that trouble begins. Because if abilities to detect emotion and humanity in the context of written communication are not exercised or deemed unimportant, people will stop looking for them in real life.

Trained in 120-character communication, pauses, and punctuation, all the things designed over hundreds of years to enhance interpersonal communications are discarded. Synonyms, antonyms, and adjectives are becoming impediments instead. It's supposed to take a while to write something deemed important. The longer it takes to compose thoughts is more time for reason to take hold. Haste makes waste. Haste allows a high schooler to send a threat to her school which gets her expelled and criminal charges being filed. The intuitive ease of use allows apps to cash in on impulsivity. When has there ever been a positive connotation to the word "impulsive"? *It was an impulse buy. Sorry, I kissed you on an impulse. Impulsively, I punched that guy.* Steadily, checks on human impulses are being eroded.

Later in this book there will be more about certain parts of the Bill of Rights of the US Constitution, specifically the right to be secure in persons, places, and things. It's argued the internet is a necessity for this life, which invariably collides and becomes confused with a basic legal right. US citizens essentially have the right to act as they please, as long as it doesn't impugn on the basic rights of others to life, liberty, and the pursuit of happiness.

All laws in the United States can be attributed to the government's attempt to protect those rights. In the absence of laws governing a large portion of citizens' everyday lives, there's a whole lot of responsibility coming with that. A US citizen's freedom is tied to these aforementioned rights, and also to the absence of laws dictating how to go about their lives.

George Washington, in his farewell address from public life, cautioned that exercise of these unalienable rights cannot be sustained without a good moral base. He referred to the pillars of religion and morality rising from the base of happiness: "In vain would that man claim the tribute of patriotism, who should labor to subvert these pillars of human happiness?" Religion of any form isn't for everyone, and that's just fine. But a sense of morality, right and wrong, is something that can be agreed on.

The basic distinction between right and wrong, a code of conduct held by people or a group, is absolutely necessary in order to enjoy and protect freedoms of any kind.

The easiest example of the erosion of morality colliding with a cherished right is the current Second Amendment debate. This is not an argument for or against the Second Amendment, as this will not advance the topic of internet safety. It is merely a timely example of the point needing to be made.

At the center of debate is the private civilian ownership of the AR-15 and other repeating firearms. The AR-15, as it is known today, has been available to regular folks since 1977, but was originally patented in 1959. Today, they number in estimates of five to ten million of over three hundred million guns in private ownership today pursuant to the exercise of the Second Amendment.

But as of late, calls for the banning of this gun have increased proportionately with the amount of mass shootings occurring at a regular, increasing pace from the 1990s onward. So if these AR-15s have been around since before the current surge of mass shootings, what's changed?

Taking the guns out of the equation, for the sake of argument, look at a recent incident when a man showed up in a Chinese school and killed eight kids with a knife. This is not the first time these knife attacks have happened in that country. China heavily restricts private gun ownership so what happens is the resort to the use of knives, explosives, and even poison to kill innocent people.

No matter the weapon used, the upsurge in people executing innocents is a serious symptom of the progressively eroding value of human life, and it's a worldwide, human phenomenon. Going further, it's not just the breathing and heart-beating part of life. The dwindling supply of empathy, kindness, and any inkling of polite discourse with others has taken society to the point of intolerance for anything or anyone unlike themselves. This erodes all of our freedom, which various dictionaries define as, in similar wording, as "the ability to act, speak, and think as one pleases without fear of hindrance or restraint."

The internet was envisioned to be the world's largest public library, with access to information to and for all. Information that was meant to be digested and leave a person still free to make up their own minds and reach their own conclusions. But the internet has become something much different than a library in terms of personal control. A person at a library has complete and total control over what information they choose to consult because it's a series of physical acts—from getting to the library, to asking the librarian for their input, digging through a card catalog, locating the resource, checking it out, and, finally, reading it. With a query on an internet search engine, what information comes back to the user is controlled by algorithms *designed and implemented by somebody else.*

Add to this the comparative culture of social media—the measuring of one's situation to another's results in the blaming of others for their own woes, and the desire to inflict hurt on those perceived wrongs through bullets, knives, or pressure-cooker bombs.

Governments in the United States have a dismal record when it comes to legislating morality. Prohibition comes to mind as the biggest failure at the federal level. These laws only work with the consent of the governed to live by those codes. It's an example in our democratic experiment that proved that the free will of people cannot, and should not, be legislated in the context of certain types of morality.

A prime example of this is adult mainstream pornography. Other than zoning laws preventing strip clubs and porn theaters from being next to churches and schools, they're perfectly legal, as are skin magazines. Before the internet, a person had to take overt, deliberate physical action to partake in pornography—subscribe to the magazines, go beyond the curtain in the back of the movie store, drive to the theater or club, and buy a ticket or pay the cover.

Just because the internet makes it easier to consume adult pornography isn't going to move the government to take action, and it shouldn't. The steps it does take to prevent children from being provided with it, such as Texas' Provide Harmful Material to a Minor statute, is only a misdemeanor, and most states take the same avenue with it. Pornography is a powerful grooming tool used by suspects to lure children, and this grooming tool is legislated by a minor misdemeanor. So, when it comes to the internet, people cannot count on the government to protect vulnerable people like children from it.

Another reason government action falls short of protecting children is a sad but easily understandable one. Crimes against children (CAC) divisions in law enforcement agencies are revenue negative. They don't make any money.

Instead, they cost vast sums in equipment and training, with no hope of recouping that cost, as is the case with vice squads through asset seizures. And if an agency is strapped for manpower in other areas, one of the first places looked at are the investigative units. These staffers by nature are self-motivators and adept at getting tasks done and on time. And when it comes to reassignment of CAC investigators, it's done very quietly. This is because there is no moral explanation for reassigning a CAC investigator to any division other than the CAC itself.

And it's done with the grudging consent of the CAC investigators because they want some hope of returning to the work they feel called to do, and nobody wants to cause their beloved police agency any negative public impressions.

Another facet to consider is the money. A good amount comes from the federal government, but the amount of funding hasn't increased with the rate of the problem.[1] In the last ten years, the funding is relatively the same. In fact, the act providing the funding was set at sixty million dollars a year, but has never been fully funded since its passing in 2008. It's never reached over half that sixty million dollars. So, of the money received, administrative costs (salaries and benefits for folks keeping a large, complicated, nationwide effort moving), public relations, grant reporting, and investigative database needs take up a sizable chunk. Another large portion is spent on dealing with turnover due to burnout. The average service time of an online exploitation investigator is two to four years. The nature of the investigations leaves them mentally and emotionally unable to continue, so new investigators need to be trained.

With full funding, the training for new investigators would stay ahead of attrition and add to the number of personnel working online exploitation. Instead, there is less than full funding added to annual budget changes. Law enforcement leaders find it difficult, if not impossible, to plan for any long-term strategic initiatives.

What this is meant to reinforce is prevention and mitigation of online predatory behavior cannot solely the responsibility of law enforcement. It has to be everybody's responsibility.

Because evil cannot be legislated out of existence. It can only be stood against.

It's easy to understand the motivation of hackers targeting a site like Ashley Madison. This site's purpose was to hook people up with extramarital affairs. To hack that site and dump subscriber data was seen as an act of karma by many.

But hackers of the same ilk turned their attention to sites like Club Penguin, a Disney-owned site for children aged six to fourteen. Over four million email addresses and IP login data were stolen and released online. Data identifying real children was freely accessible to people with a sexual interest in children. There was enough data to engineer passwords that could be used to take over accounts and blackmail kids into producing explicit material.

The question now seems to be "Can this be done?" rather than "Should this be done?" Nobody is totally safe online. There is no reigning in the mob mentality of the internet. Just like in the aftermath of a natural disaster, the absence of any real laws or precedent made it very easy to loot the hell out of the internet. What's been done is the world's largest shopping mall, but with sex shops set up next to daycares and churches.

It used to be if a person wasn't near their office desk phone or home to receive a call, nobody could get into contact until that person came home or back from lunch. In the same vein, before caller ID boxes and answering machines, nobody had any idea if anyone tried to call while out. Then came pagers. With cell phones, twenty-four/seven contact quickly became the norm.

Whatever feelings you may have about devices and social media, their use is expected now. In fact, just to publish a book, an author is expected to provide all social media and website information, to be evaluated on the potential of a platform to sell this book. It's not possible to be the cliche recluse writer anymore. J. D. Salinger, Harper Lee, and the like, in this day, could not merely spit out a book to a publisher and rely on them to sell it. Now, a hybrid recluse may be possible if someone is hired to run the social media and website side of this business.

But even then, podcasts, these mini television and radio shows anybody with a couple of good microphones, cameras, and an internet connection can produce, have become a powerful tool for people to connect with their favorite anybody. People, especially children, may say they don't care what other people think, but the insecurities brought on by negative comments are epidemic. They do care, because people are wired to be social beings with the need to be accepted and loved by people deemed important. Online followers, specifically the amount of said followers, have become important enough to be popularity contests among children.

Coolness is equated to followers. So when confronted by someone or a group who doesn't like what's said, what's worn, or what was for lunch, it can actually affect how one's day goes.

Years ago, a news story could be viewed and conclusions drawn based upon the information received. Who shot J. R.? Did Armstrong and company really land on the moon? Was Nixon lying? Did O. J. kill Nicole and Ron? One could turn the television off and be totally in a vacuum of thought to make up their own mind. These days, whether it's realized or not, opinions are shaped by the first two or three posts in the newsfeed. Instead of picking apart things, the event is absorbed through somebody else's lens and a different conclusion reached had it not been for that online resource.

Everyone, especially young people, needs to understand what is happening when they use social media and the internet. There needs to be an emphasis on informed consent, being fully aware of what one is getting into when they use these services. Social media does not, and has never, operated this way. How long a particular user lingers on a picture or how often they visit a site or profile is logged into that user's own personal data profile. Consider a relationship break up. It seems the ex's content is just forced through their newsfeed. It's because that user's little niche in the vast digital ocean has noticed a change in behavior. And if this change decreases use of the platform, it's going to be very aggressive to get that user back. It's like going fishing with a friend. That friend is catching fish, and the other hasn't had a bite all day. Eventually the other will ask what the fish are biting on. And much like a dog running through all of the tricks it knows when it doesn't know what its human wants, social media does the same thing. If the ex's content isn't working, maybe it'll push political stuff and progress all the way down to a cute puppy dog until it gets that user engaged again.

Informed consent for social media is very simple. One has to understand they're being manipulated and spied upon. Consider Locard's Principle of Exchange. This principle pertains to crime scene investigation techniques. Locard holds that a criminal brings something to a crime scene and leaves with something from it. In other words, coming into contact with anything changes it, even if it's the slightest ripple. Nobody can say with any reasonable certainty they weren't changed after reading something online. Anybody who says they weren't is delusional.

To Recap:

- Freedoms of any kind, including the internet, require a solid moral base.
- Government is woefully ill-designed to combat online child exploitation on its own.
- Don't let others do the thinking—for the child or the stakeholder.

NOTE

1. Keller, Michael H., and Gabriel Dance. "The Internet is Overrun with Images of Child Sexual Abuse. What Went Wrong?" *New York Times*, September 28, 2019. https://www.nytimes.com/interactive/2019/09/28/us/child-sex-abuse.html.

3

THE HOME IS NOT A DEMOCRACY, AND SCHOOL SAFETY SEARCHES

In this chapter, it's time to dive into what's needed to be effective in the fight against online exploitation in the home and, the second place kids spend the most time, at school. Before getting too far into the detection and prevention of online crimes against children, it is important to note this: The home is not a democracy. Parents need to view it as a dictatorship from the top down, but not in the authoritarian, one-way sense of the word. There needs to be an atmosphere of love and respect between parent and child, but the parent needs to understand there is no such thing as total privacy when it comes to devices and the data they hold in the hands of juvenile children.

Every search conducted by parents in their homes regarding the safety and security of their children is deemed reasonable by the very fact it's their home and their children. The only people who will deem it unreasonable are children because of the simple fact that they are children and don't know any better. But parents do, and by virtue of their example as interference, successful parents in the digital arena get into their children's business and stay there, dug in on the front lines.

To some parents, this is a pretty obvious stance because it's how they were raised. But there are parents who grew up without effective models to emulate and want to do better with their own families, so they need a source of authority by which to act, much like the statutes governing law enforcement and school officials. The Bill of Rights is a good place to start by examining the actual wording of the Fourth Amendment. The genius of the Fourth Amendment is the simple use of simple words and the order to which they were placed: "The right of people to be secure in their possessions, houses, papers, and effects, against unreasonable searches and seizures, shall not be violated, and no warrants shall issue, but upon probable cause, supported by an Oath or affirmation, and particularly describing the place to be searched and the persons or things to be seized."

It's the words "effects" and "things" which make the Fourth Amendment cover technology and devices nowhere near imagined by the Founding Fathers. The word "effects" in this context means personal belongings and possessions, which includes electronic devices. "Things" is an abstract and generic term which can be applied to just about anything, including data.

Contemporary discussions of the Fourth Amendment seem to center on the privacy issue, equating the terms "security" with "privacy." It's also the first line stakeholders throw at law enforcement when defending their lack of digital diligence in their kids' lives: "We respect our kids' privacy, so that's why we didn't ever go looking in their phones" or "We'd never betray our kid's trust and privacy."

Stakeholders are often taken aback by assertions that kids have no rights in the home and are hesitant to just barge their rooms and go through their stuff. It's understandable. After all, it's not something parents had to do when their children were young, compliant, and worshipped the ground parents walked on. It's a recent development as the children get older, more independent, and think for themselves. At this point, it's time to remember what was discussed earlier—laying out expectations and consequences for not adhering to them, and regular discussion/confrontation of things they encounter online as methods of reinforcement of desired behavior.

And herein lies any justification a parent might need to lean on in these times. The expectations? Those are laws of the home. Failure to obey them constitutes a family crime. And just like an act contrary to the peace and dignity of any state in the United States, both must be investigated.

In the law enforcement world, there are consent searches and probable cause searches. Consent searches are those conducted with the property owner's consent. Consent can be verbally given (weakest form of consent) or written consent (strongest form). Consent can be revoked at any time by the grantor, and they must be effectively able to do so. Probable cause searches are done when there are facts and circumstances which would lead a reasonable and prudent person to conclude a crime has been or is about to be committed. Probable cause is extremely important as it is the foundation of policing in a democratic, free society.

In schools, things are slightly different. Before going any further, laws governing school searches vary widely from the national level to state to state. Some jurisdictions have very strict protections in place; others are more permissive. It is prudent to know and understand these laws. And in addition to these local laws, school district regulations can go further in both permissiveness and restrictions as long as they don't go afoul of the laws. Readers are strongly urged to abide by all laws, rules, and regulations in place wherever they are.

What's being advocated here is taking full advantage of being in the right place at the right time when it comes to another legal principle called the plain view doctrine. This is an exception to the Fourth Amendment warrant requirement provided the discovery of evidence was made when lawfully present to view it in plain view, a lawful right of access, and the incriminating nature of the evidence is readily apparent.

Supreme Court decisions, such as *New Jersey vs. T.L.O.*, hold searches conducted in schools by school employees as based upon the reasonableness standard, or whether the search is reasonable under the circumstances of the search. The meaning of reasonable depends on the type of search being conducted and if that search was appropriate to the facts and circumstances at the time.

The reasonableness standard is a lower requirement than probable cause, but more than a gut feeling or a mere hunch. The school official must have an articulable reason to believe the student has committed, or is committing, an action which is subject to disciplinary infraction. In other words, the search is justified at the outset because of a belief it will uncover evidence of the suspected action. It must also be an appropriate response to the level of offense suspected, and the age and sex of the student is yet another item on the checklist of reasonableness.

What makes cell phone searches tricky is what's being searched: data. And this is way different than a backpack for drugs, weapons, or vaping equipment. It's because a cell phone holds so much information, and much of it has nothing to do with school business. These "privacies of life" the Supreme Court refers to can lead a school administration to proceed with large amounts of caution when it comes to policies and actions concerning data on cell phones, either to avoid conflict with students' parents, or from a "no harm, no foul" approach to avoid liabilities.

The problem with that kind of approach is that schools have an overwhelming interest in ensuring not only the safety of the school itself, but individual student safety (concerns specific to a particular student) as well.

After all, one student's problem, say, with an online predator situation, can and will easily spread to others.

As an example, a thirty-three-year-old man was arrested for violations of Texas' Online Solicitation of a Minor and Possession of Child Pornography statutes. This man, who was also an elementary school music teacher, used two online female personas to solicit his former male students after they graduated to middle school. Over the course of two years, this prolific online predator moved through each victim's friends lists and eventually had over three hundred unique victims in all fifty states. In a small town in Idaho, one member of the school's baseball team fell victim, but not before he passed the suspect female online persona onto the rest of the twelve-man roster. In a military school, a whole barracks room was affected. This case will be further explored in this text in another chapter.

Earlier in this book, it was put forward that educators should not be solely focused on disciplining a student for a cell phone infraction. Granted, some students just don't care about rules or consequences for breaking them. Students not caring about certain rules concerning yelling in the hallways or chewing gum isn't new. But what's universal among students is the reliance, or even addiction, to their phones, so therefore what they're risking device confiscation for must be important.

Another case dealt with a twelve-year-old boy caught using his phone during a statewide mandated test. This test is so important that the students' school lives are disrupted with special testing periods, with emails sent to parents suggesting a good breakfast and earlier bedtime the night before. Students being disruptive during this test are dealt with swiftly, and punishments are heavy. So this student risked his freedom to answer text messages. The teacher saw it and took the phone away from the child.

On the way back to her desk, she observed sexually explicit text messages on the home screen. These texts indicated the sender was getting on a plane to come and meet the child. Further, the messages were of an adult nature, clearly written by an adult. This teacher could have just powered down the phone, shamed the child for breaking the rules, but instead she asked that all important question: Why?

She alerted a counselor, who called the parents, who called law enforcement. Specially trained undercover chat operators took over the text messaging just as the suspect got on a plane to come have sex with this boy. It turned out he was an airline pilot who used his employee benefits to fly for free. The child's parents were supposed to go to a party that night and leave the boy alone at home, and the adult male was planning to drive to the boy's house and sexually assault him. Instead, undercover law enforcement watched him get off the plane, drive to and check into a hotel, and then drive to the boy's home where he was arrested in the cul-de-sac.

This teacher saved that boy's mental and, quite possibly, physical life. Courts have consistently ruled in favor of student safety overriding any concerns about data privacy. But increasingly these rulings are becoming more and more restrictive concerning *searches*. But in the preceding example, the teacher had a lawful right to be where she was, and with lawful access to the cell phone. Plainly evident on the open screen was the incriminating nature of the text messages. She took advantage of the situation much like a police officer would on a traffic stop when he sees guns, drugs, or other contraband plainly evident—right place, right time, and lawfully present.

One of the questions asked in the first chapter was: Are stakeholders aware of what children face online?

If a stakeholder doesn't know what their child is doing online, they don't have all the clues.

Catching things like a child talking to a habitual sex offender online early means the difference between a few months of psychotherapy to undo some mental warping or a lifetime without the child because they are dead. In the business of defending against online predators, There's the death of innocence, of security, the loss of a true childhood, all of which are a lifetime sentence.

Is it too hard or maybe outside of a stakeholder's business to deal with?

A short course in law enforcement procedures will provide some common ground in problem-solving. Many parents don't normally go into their children's rooms and surreptitiously check their electronic devices unless some unusual event, like the child was caught sneaking out or in, or gone without parental knowledge when this hadn't happened before. What if the child is accidentally caught taking explicit photos of themselves when the bathroom door wasn't locked? What if parents were called to the school because a stranger tried to pick up the child, who was then detained by the school cops and it was discovered that stranger had been in a clandestine online relationship with my child?

All these behaviors are clues. They are clues that something has gone wrong in a kid's life. That "something" may have begun innocently enough, but cyber-criminals are experts in getting kids (and adults) to trust, then taking advantage of that trust.

Sneaking out at night is against the curfew laws, not to mention household laws. Producing child pornography by taking nude self-pictures is against these household laws and that of the state's. Online solicitation of a minor is against the law in all fifty states. A crime has been committed.

Searches and seizures of all a child's belongings, including their devices, is most certainly warranted. Children make mistakes, and part of parenting is to ensure the mistakes they make won't jeopardize their safety or other peoples' safety.

An educator's gut-level instincts that recognize a change in a child's behavior need to be investigated; what steps can be taken that's within school policy to investigate that?

Are all stakeholders willing to protect children from cyber-criminals by getting into their children's online life and stay there?

To Recap:

- The home is not a democracy. Every search conducted is deemed reasonable because the parent is the parent and the child is a child.
- Stakeholders should take full advantage of the plain view doctrine and capitalize on being in the right place at the right time.
- Ask the all-important question: Why?

4

TRUTH AND EFFICIENCY
ON THE INTERNET

Think about how military recruitment handles itself these days. The commercials are startlingly combat-realistic, like the *Call of Duty* franchise, something different from the recruitment programs of the past. "Be all that you can be," "The few, the proud, the Marines," "Aim High"—all focused on the intrinsic attributes of the proud US military tradition. Shiny uniforms, formation drills, free education, room and board, world travel—these shifted focus from the military's purpose to kill the nation's enemies. World travel includes whatever hell hole was deemed vital to national security. Digitized warfare on gaming systems gives kids more than enough ideas of what military service really entails.

There's no longer a need to gloss over young adults killing and destroying things, either directly or indirectly through their actions. It's no secret the military uses the immense popularity of warfare role-playing games as a recruitment tool, sending gaming teams to gamer competitions as an outreach tool. It allows the military to be more truthful about the job.

Child predators are also more truthful about who they are, thanks to the sheer number of potential victims the internet provides. This negates the necessity of long-term grooming to develop a victim into a "sure thing." If the predator sends a hundred sexually explicit messages, and a handful of children respond, he gets what he wants. Even if the child receives such a message and ignores it, there's still Locard's Principle. The child carries something away from that encounter, and it's not anything positive whatsoever.

These messages, often called "creeper messages," are so common, most children have received one or several. For this reason, asking a child if they've ever received one is an excellent starting point for a conversation about online safety. A creeper message is defined as a message from someone the child doesn't know, saying something the child found uncomfortable, and likely had a picture attachment of pornographic content or a request for sexually explicit material.

There are over seven billion people on the face of this planet. For simplicity's sake, figure half of them have some sort of regular access to the internet. This leaves three and a half billion people. If a stakeholder's child answers yes about creeper messages, that child was chosen out of those billions of possible recipients. In that context, it's a sinking feeling of a loved one being singled out.

One of the reasons predators send these messages so freely is because most children won't say anything out of fear of getting in trouble for receiving it. But if a child knows they can speak up without fear of the stakeholder, how many more actionable reports would law enforcement receive? It may wind up like a recent case of a child in Miami, Florida, reporting a creeper message. Investigators in Florida traced it to a residence in Houston, Texas. Texas investigators were able to secure a search warrant. What they found was a middle-aged male who'd been sending messages like those for years, and with hundreds of victims.

How many less victims would he have had if his first one was empowered by a stakeholder to say something?

To Recap:

- The readily available information on anything via the internet has made it easier to be truthful about any topic.
- Children hesitate to tell stakeholders about an uncomfortable online experience out of fear they will be blamed for it.
- Open lines of communication between stakeholder and child is essential.

5

NOTHING IS BETTER
THAN THE TRUTH

Let's go to the second question highlighted in the introduction of this book: *Is it too hard or maybe outside of a stakeholder's business to deal with?*

Clearly, the "it" in this question is whatever problem is found in a child's online postings on social media or by a search of their devices. It's always the fervent hope of stakeholders to not find any clues pointing to a problem, such as a clandestine relationship with an inappropriate person or a mental/emotional problem destroying the child's hope and belief in a good future.

A big part of the proactive approach advocated here is to be prepared ahead of a crisis. Outside of online child exploitation issues, the age-old problems schoolchildren have faced for years—pestering; being made fun of for clothing, hairstyles, or the trailer park or rundown apartment complex they live in; body styles and shapes; basically anything drawing out the detestable behaviors in schools since the dawn of time—have exploded in sheer scope given the twenty-four/seven presence of technology.

In the pre-technology era, there was downtime after school from tormentors making fun of clothes, hair, or anything else that was fair game. That down time gave a chance to consult with siblings and parents for next moves. That's not so anymore. The torment and bad behavior now continues via social networks. Even turning off the phone offers little escape. It has to be turned back on again. There is no tactical retreat for sanity and reason to reestablish itself.

Children are mentally exhausted from all of this. There's just so much coming from all directions. It's no surprise that some teenagers resort to self-harming behaviors like cutting, self-destructive behaviors such as drug and alcohol abuse, or, worse, suicide. It's not uncommon for law enforcement to conduct forensic examinations of personal devices in order to answer lingering questions for the curve nobody saw coming.

What's typically learned is the child suffered for a long time through the typical teenage mess of life, but they made the mistake of confiding to another child thought to be a friend, text messaging back and forth. The other child capitalized on the misfortune and screenshotted the messages, sharing them with others at their mutual school. What it boils down to is too much information in the hands of the wrong people.

But as despicable as the behavior is, it's a common way for the information to get in the hands of the right people. The finger pointing, jeers, the clusters of students around a cellular device, and snippets of conversations picked up by educators in the halls should be used as reports to those at the educational institution equipped to handle such dismalities. Once the child is behind closed doors with a counselor, they're in the presence of someone willing to listen, and often that's all it takes to get an issue in the open.

Information is like a shopping coupon. If used after the expiration date, it's value is worthless. The timeliness of information is just as powerful as the content. Online exploitation investigators do internet safety presentations at schools. It's a great idea to have school counselors on hand during these. The content rings true to those living online nightmares. They wear the heavy emotional burdens on their faces, making them easy to spot.

These presentations are given with three goals in mind: to get the information into the children's and stakeholders' hands, to foster better decision making, and, finally, to provide an opportunity for the child to outcry about abuse. This author has provided this safety training to over forty thousand children and adults. In doing so, a few conclusions were made regarding such training and its availability in schools.

States vary with regards to requirements of internet safety curriculum. Many states only require safety materials be made available online as a resource for educators to use. Some states have implemented mandatory curriculum requirements, but these vary widely as to what is covered and how long is allotted to cover it. Others require some form of training once a school year but don't specify what or how. Further, some states don't have reporting mechanisms in place to ensure it's been done.

There's much more uniformity with sex education requirements, with an extensive curriculum to go with it. This is understandable as it is a much more longstanding issue. Internet and social media concerns are much more Johnny-come-lately. Both issues present huge implications on students' lives, and as such should be treated equally both in time devoted and requirements. This is an issue at the states' education agency level for policy makers and politicians.

So what can stakeholders do to help? All can demand and support changes through interactions with policy makers. While parents and guardians can control the frequency and content of their education efforts, teachers are encouraged to seek out and seize more teachable moments throughout their school days on appropriate safety topics. However, making the technology mandatory to be a successful student today makes educational systems responsible for internet safety being part of the curriculum, so clearly this is the ideal accomplishment.

In differentiating a proactive versus reactive approach, proactive means the stakeholder thinks things through before they happen. Reactive means the stakeholders react to the crisis as it's unfolding. Think of it like train travel. Which is preferable? Boarding a stopped train at a predetermined time in the safe environment of a train station (proactive), or boarding alongside the tracks onto a moving train, trying to grab whatever handhold possible, hoping not to be pulled under the wheels (reactive)?

Life, by its very nature, is often composed of both proactive and reactive situations. For instance, accidents cause a role that is reactive. But a proactive mode is needed when it comes to cyber-security of children. Part of the reason why parents and educators tend to adopt a "hands-off" attitude to children's social media and devices is because the parent doesn't feel comfortable enough to understand how these devices work.

Or perhaps it's an ignorance thing, such as not knowing the devices have certain capabilities. In short, there's a huge knowledge gap. This can be overcome. A little investment of time on the internet will bring tons of practical information on the usage of most devices. Most companies have committed to making their devices "intuitive" to use in the first place, so this should ease stakeholders' use of these devices.

No Apple product comes with an instruction manual. In addition, Steve Jobs wanted his creations to be so easy to use a child could do it, and they do. Technology is like a hammer. A common tool used to join things together or hang up a picture, but it can also be used to break into a house and, like the internet, it has good uses and bad uses. People can do anything after watching a YouTube video on the subject, and that includes protecting children.

Getting back to the question about if it's too hard to deal with: a resounding *no* is the answer. Take into account all parents have gone through to get to this point in the parenting journey. Maybe a bedrest pregnancy or a tough delivery. Childhood disease and illness, colic, jaundice, toilet training, broken bones, surgeries, the child's emotional pain of not making a baseball or dance team. Rejections of all types.

For educators, there are similar hard moments: the last day of kindergarten or the last day of fifth grade, hoping the job of preparing them for the next stage was done. As parents and educators, *failure is not an option.*

There is one thing that all the past examples mentioned have in common: they're reactive in nature. Sure, there could be some preemptive thought as to what would be done if little Sally or Joe landed wrong on the trampoline and broke their forearm. There's a plan in place that's pretty brainless: Take them to the hospital, pay the copay, get a cast, listen to itching complaints for the next six weeks. Most things in life are reactive in nature. An event happens, and it's dealt with.

Technology and children are not the kind of problems to handle reactively. It can't be.

Every ounce of trouble, frustration, and embarrassment that could conceivably be caused to a parent or educator is worth the ultimate goal: keeping children safe from cyber-criminals and bullies. If the truth is known of what they're doing, texting, posting, and experimenting with, then there's a better chance of keeping them safe.

This is the only hope of being proactive: knowing the children and parents spending enough time with them to forge deep relationships. Educators and parents alike should share wisdom about life and people. Homeroom or advisory teachers should spend a few moments discussing a news article about technology abuses of any type that's relevant to the child's life; coupled with parental efforts at home, this makes open and permissive discussions about online exploitation possible. And that is a huge part of the overall strategy discussed in further chapters in this book.

To Recap:

- Being prepared ahead of a crisis is the cornerstone of proactive approaches.
- The typical bad behaviors of youth should be used to get information in the hands of the right people.
- Forming ever deeper relationships between children and stakeholders is key in protecting them online.

6

HAMSTERS ARE RATS, AND DEVICES ARE HAMSTERS BUT STILL RATS

Imagine moving into a new home, and then a few months later, hearing the pitter-patter of rodents in the attic. This is not an uncommon occurrence in home ownership, and calling a pest control company cures the issue. Then, the youngest child wants a pet hamster and that wish is granted. It might be lost, the amount of money spent to get rid of rodents and then paying to have one live in the house. This is not unlike purchasing a smartphone. While keeping track of a child's location and talking to them, all of that being good stuff, they're capable of using apps counterintuitive to what stakeholders teach about their personal safety and emotional growth.

Hamsters are rats, and devices are hamsters but still rats. Following this rat theme, it's interesting to take a lesson from basic psychology. In the 1930s, psychologist B. F. Skinner conducted a series of experiments regarding incentive and reward behavior. He constructed an enclosed box with a food pellet feeder controlled by a small lever. Then he let a rat loose in the box. As rats do, it inspected the new environment and bumped into the lever. A food pellet was made available to eat. Eventually, the rat figured out hitting the lever fed it.

Skinner deduced the environment has effects on those in that environment. While this is a simplification of his work, if one constructs the right conditions, any desired behavior can be brought about using incentive and reward. Fast forward to now to the digital box. The study of incentive to use digital applications and the rewards keeping users coming back is called behavior design.

A prominent figure in behavior design is B. J. Fogg of Stanford University. As early as the late 1990s, before the current tech revolution, he conducted experiments proving people could be induced to use a computer for longer periods of time if they felt the computer was helpful in the past. His conclusion was as simple as it was predictive.

Applications could be designed using psychological principles to make people do things they wouldn't ordinarily do. One of Fogg's former students went on to help found Instagram.[1]

Now that it's understood social media applications are designed using principles of human psychological frailties, add that to the hyperdrive of manipulation in a predatory relationship. It's two trains colliding head on.

A favorite place for teenagers is their room. They are physically alone but not mentally. Mindlessly scrolling through a Twitter feed, watching crazy stunts on YouTube and TikTok, zipping through things. It seems they're so afraid of missing something, but that something really has no bearing on their lives at that moment, or maybe never at all.

In schools, educators see them, groups of five or six, sitting on bleachers or in the cafeteria. They actually know each other or are at least aware there are people around. Every single one is engrossed in their phones. What's being witnessed is the slow, wheezing death of interpersonal interactions. The gentle art of investing in someone else and having them do the same.

The Social Network is a movie chronicling the genesis of Facebook. There's one scene in which Mark Zuckerberg is asked if he knows a particular girl and if she has a boyfriend. Mark, at first very much annoyed, says people don't walk around with a sign saying what their relationship status is. And that leads to the ah-hah moment to code the relationship status into his fledgling Facebook.

How many people decide whether to pursue a love interest based upon what they see online? It definitely can be argued it's just simpler, easier, this way. Maybe it's cheapened. Things easily attained quickly produce dissatisfaction, making the person wonder if there's something better out there, and it's just so easy to look for it. In these days of instant gratification, people shy away from the requisite amount of time to find out if that other person is their brand of crazy, and vice versa.

Children need to be taught to be responsible for the unprecedented access to power technology provides. In much the same way they're told to stand for the national anthem, to be quiet in church, to hold the door open for old people, girls, women, basically everybody in general. Good digital citizenship needs to be taught while the parenting and educating generation still hold a lot of the keys to their futures.

To Recap:

- Devices and social networks are designed to incentivize their use.
- Combining the incentive to use and the manipulation of a predatory relationship set up the inevitable train wreck to follow.
- If the child has access to a device, they are not really alone.

NOTES

1. Leslie, Ian. "The Scientists Who Make Apps Addictive." *The Economist 1843 Magazine*, October/November 2016. https://www.1843magazine.com/features/the-scientists-who-make-apps-addictive.

7

PICK UP THAT DEVICE

Online predators aren't the only concern stakeholders can catch by in-specting their child's device.

Remember, a child's digital device is like an online diary in all respects. What do depressed people do? They look up and consume sad material. A trend like that can be caught by examining the device's playlists. This is the modern-day version of parents checking their kid's record collection for parental advisories and looking for the written lyrics on the cassette jackets. Depression isn't the only topic that can be identified by song lyrics. Sexual identity issues, unrequited love, and the glorification of violence are all important concerns.

Kids who are withdrawn through depression or social anxiety seek es-cape, and often it's in their devices. Checking screen-time averages can track increases and decreases in device usage. Depressed children spend large amounts of time trying to figure themselves out online. A stakeholder can see what applications the child is using the most.

A stakeholder's time is limited. They can quickly get to the heart of the matter through another data point contained in screen time monitoring, and that's called a pickup. A pickup is a measurement of how many times a device is picked up and used. Pickups are important because they also track what the user does with the phone after it's picked up. Which apps are used directly after pickup can point to what the child is most concerned about. If a child is going to a messaging application after each pickup, the questions are who are they talking to and why. Perhaps there is a child predator at the other end of the line, or it could be a troubled relationship or crisis with a friend or significant other. Whether it's an Apple or an Android device, both have applications and settings that will track screen time usage and what's been done with that device recently. Checking in with these screen-time applications can also be taught to the child as a form of self-assessment—perhaps they are not aware of how much time they actually spend on their devices. Stakeholders shouldn't be immune from appraisals of their own device usage either.

Use the technology against itself. This method surely beats random searching on the child's device. Even if a child has hidden a particular app from the home screen, that action won't keep the app from being monitored in screen time and pickups. In one particular case, a stakeholder located an application designed to hide media files and discovered her daughter's cache of self-produced pornography she'd been sending to an online predator.

It takes a lot of courage to go looking for something a stakeholder doesn't want to find. In the next chapter, the discussion turns to some methodologies child predators use to bring into more focus why regular device searches are so important.

To Recap:

- A child's device is the modern-day diary.
- Metrics the device keeps on its own should be used to identify concerns.
- Use the technology against itself.

8

METHODOLOGY OF THE CHILD PREDATOR

It's time to introduce the felony sex criminal who is after children. It's not enough to know they exist. News articles seldom lay down exactly what these people have done, in the interests of brevity and decency.

To introduce these criminals is to introduce people familiar to family life. These defendants performed everyday, necessary roles in society—the same roles everybody has in orbit around their lives, until the criminals' real motives were uncovered and brought to justice. Nobody likes to think these monsters could be someone invited into their lives. But they were masters of deception and fooled everyone until they didn't.

Case One: The middle school teacher who sent a video of himself masturbating to an undercover officer's fourteen-year-old persona. He then sent "her" child pornography in an effort to make "her" feel comfortable sending him nude selfies. He was arrested in his classroom after school was out for the day.

Case Two: The elementary school teacher, a preferential sex offender fixated on pubescent and post-pubescent males ages eleven to fourteen, who followed his male students silently on social media until they were sexually interesting to him. He then posed online as a former female student they all knew and solicited the boys for nude pictures and videos of themselves. This man, who had been charged with the protection and education of children, did nothing but cause chaos in the lives of over three hundred young boys.

Case Three: The middle school teacher tackled in his front yard during a search warrant service because he masturbated in a webcam session to a twelve-year-old girl in another state.

Case Four: An airline pilot who used his employment benefits to fly from Minnesota to Houston to have sex with an eleven-year-old boy he'd met on social media.

Case Five: Another airline pilot found with over seventeen terabytes of child pornography. If all his pictures and the videos frame-by-frame were printed out onto paper, they'd fill twenty semi-truck trailers front to back with stacks of paper. This pilot was completely and utterly obsessed with the sexual abuse of children to amass such a collection, undoubtedly to the point of distraction in his everyday life.

Case Six: The church youth pastor who seduced a troubled teenage girl and collected bestiality child pornography as a side pursuit.

Case Seven: A guy so eaten up with a child pornography addiction he urinated in plastic milk jugs so he didn't have to leave his computer with the pornographic images.

Case Eight: A well-respected orthopedic surgeon applauded for his pro bono work for less fortunate citizens, who used that as a cover to locate and identify troubled youth and sexually exploit them. The search warrant execution scene video of his seventeen-thousand-square-foot home took two hours to shoot.

Case Nine: A guy who sought shelter during one of Houston's famous hurricanes with his friend's family, only to have their son wake up to him masturbating in front of his face as he recorded it using his cell phone. The perpetrator checked into a local motel and shot himself in the bathroom the day before sentencing.

Case Ten: A guy who sold sessions online for people to watch him sexually assault his five-year-old daughter.

Case Eleven: A man who showed to pick up what he thought was a thirteen-year-old girl during an undercover operation, with rope, duct tape, alcohol, pills, and trash bags in the back of his SUV.

Case Twelve: A school district police officer assigned to a middle school campus had an iPhone full of pornographic images of juvenile girls the same age as the students on his campus.

Case Thirteen: A police officer who worked in an underserved community offered to pay a juvenile teenage girl for sex.

Case Fourteen: A woman's ex-boyfriend solicited that woman's teenage daughter for sex and the two exchanged sexually explicit images of one another.

Case Fifteen: A lifeguard at a community pool had sexual contact with juvenile girls who utilized the pool.

Case Fifteen: An elementary school teacher who sought out and exchanged child pornography online of children the same age as he taught.

Case Sixteen: A middle school teacher who collected child pornography and wrote sexually explicit stories about a teacher having sex with his female students.

Case Seventeen: A professional photographer known for his family photo sessions collected child pornography in his spare time.

It's important to get rid of the most common misperceptions about the type of people who try to prey upon children through the "open door" that technology often provides. Yes, there are stereotypes of internet predators. Here's a list of characteristics usually provided by middle schoolers during internet safety presentations:

- Fat white dude
- Bald white dude
- Fat bald white dude
- Cheetos dust on fingers, keyboard, mouse, and elsewhere . . .
- Nerd
- Lives with his mother
- Drives a dirty old van
- Has several cats and smells like them
- Short, fat, bald white dude
- First name Chester, last name Molester

Those stereotype offenders are out there. So are clean-cut guys, even muscular guys with sterling work records for attendance and performance. Shy or outgoing. Doctors, lawyers, priests, teachers, coaches, and other cops. Wolves aren't always obvious, and Scary Larry could literally be anyone: male, female, gay, straight, married, single, college-educated or a GED, a big bankroll or paycheck to paycheck. A good many of these folks have trouble maintaining a mature adult relationship, but some are long married in what appears to be a stable and positive relationship, perhaps even to the envy of their friends.

One of the most important things to realize is that anyway it's sliced, the problems of youth are universal and haven't changed much in principle, just in application. Cell phones and social media are used as methods of harassment, intimidation, bullying, and so on, replacing "Kick Me" signs taped to backs, wedgies, and other age-old bad behavior. These predators have lived through it already. They know what it's like to be made fun of because of one's clothes, hairstyle, what kind of car their parents drive, what neighborhood, trailer park, or apartment complex they live in, and so on. And they also know all kids are looking for someone to be nice to them and say things they're not required to say.

Parents tell children they're pretty or handsome, funny, cool to be around, but the child is thinking, *yeah right, you're my mom/dad and you have to say all that*. Or worse, the kid is not getting that support at home. Be it the former or the latter, the first time children hear that kind of positive stuff from somebody who doesn't have to say it, it's like crack cocaine, and they're hooked.

Suspects use technology to solicit kids for sex, reading a screenplay of the worst adult video ever created to the child, telling them exactly what they want to do and how they want to do it, doing things most adults wouldn't dream of doing to someone they care about. But, at its very core, that graphic language is *positive reinforcement*. Child victims often say, "He wouldn't want to do that if I wasn't attractive/hot/pretty/handsome."

Another characteristic of online sexual predators is patience. And, don't forget, they are not just talking to one child at a time. Kicking in doors on felony search warrants often finds them managing multiple conversations at the same time. They print out messages and make notes on what they want to ask the child next and how they want to say it. These bad guys research and get to know children through their social media. They find the foothold they need to drive a wedge between the child and their stakeholders.

The elementary school teacher mentioned at the beginning of this chapter successfully posed as both a juvenile female and an adult woman on the internet. He got over three hundred young boys to produce sexually explicit images and videos of themselves and send them to him. That case took over a year and half to identify nearly all of them, hundreds of interviews, accomplished by law enforcement in all fifty states and two countries overseas.

In these types of cases, usually there are all kinds of victims: clean-cut athletes and students, guys who look like slackers or bookish, disrespectful punks slumped in a chair. But in this case, all the identified victims were well adjusted, soft spoken, humble, articulate, smart, and motivated young men with roughly the same physical features. This offender was able to locate, size up, and motivate literally the same kind of boy over and over again, using nothing but social media to make that kind of assessment.

Putting it over the top, nearly every child he talked to produced pornographic images, a much higher success rate than commonly seen. So, this teacher was able to predict with nearly a 100 percent success rate the chances of getting files from a kid, just by social media research alone. That's a scary prediction of a kid's behavior made by a person who had been teaching for several years.

This is a good time to address educators as perpetrators of online child exploitation. Keep in mind, adults with a sexual interest in children will choose occupations, hobbies, or volunteer opportunities putting them in contact with children. And not just casual contact, but full on, same airspace kind of contact, the type necessary to be a successful educator. Making matters worse, these predators are often a teacher all the students and parents love, one with the most former student visitors, organizing after-hours social events to blow off steam, perhaps making sure there's a cake in the breakroom for a birthday celebration.

This makes the revelation of the monster they are one of the most devastating events on campus, tearing at the threads of an institution past the stitches. Trust among coworkers, between parent and educator, and between student and educator is damaged. Anger runs deep on all sides, leaving a school's staff reeling and an administration under siege.

By and large, principals hire their own teachers. They sign off and accept transfer educators into their institutions. And when these educators turn out to be child predators, the blame comes at them. More importantly, principals are educators themselves who've heeded the call to lead from the front. Every child coming through those doors is their own for eight or more hours a day. Besides the blame from outside, the personal angst at allowing such a person access to *their* kids is horrifying.

In one particular case, video files from a camera hidden on campus by a predator/educator capturing elementary school children changing clothes was found. While non-pornographic in nature, it's a huge violation of trust and privacy, and the principal's help was needed to identify the children.

What's important to remember is that red-flag behavior of the educator/ predator in hindsight is, by and large, ordinary behavior of a devoted educator. Going to a student's sporting event, funerals of their parents, staying after school for one-on-one tutoring, doting on favorite students, volunteering as sponsors for student clubs, and chaperoning field trips are all signs of a good teacher.

While other predators are caught and neighbors say, "I knew there was something wrong with that guy," it's rare to hear those words uttered from an educator/predator's coworkers. Stunned silence, crying, and even fainting are the reactions seen. The criminal is just that good at operating. Educator/predators are the ultimate chameleon of the predator class.

If a principal and their administration find themselves with an investigator explaining how one of their teachers was arrested that morning for child exploitation, here are some important things to keep in mind.

- Ask when the law enforcement agency's media release is coming out. Ask for time to notify school district administration so a response can be drafted and ready.
- That investigator will want access to the educator's classroom(s). They will want to confiscate computers, flash media, notebooks, and anything found of evidentiary value. Be abreast of state/local laws and district policies regarding these requests.
- The investigator is not there to make things worse. They are there to conduct as complete an investigation as possible. Bluntness is a product of timely collection of evidence, not a personality trait.
- Tend to subordinates and staff accordingly. Counselors should be available not only for students, but for teachers as well.
- Things will get worse before they get better. Think of the most egregious breach of trust a predator/educator can do, and be prepared for it.

There's a saying in our internet crime-fighting "business." On the internet, men are men and so are the women. Men often masquerade as teenage females not only to approach boys, but also girls. Despite repeated warnings not to, children blindly accept follow requests without a look-back.

For discussion's sake, it's a Friday night and a son or daughter is headed to the movies with friends. Parents know who they're with, where they are, and when they need to be picked up. After dropoff, the child takes a picture in front of the movie poster they are seeing and posts it, including a check-in at the theater. Now, this adult faking online as a child knows where the child will be for the next two to three hours. He goes to the movies too, buying a ticket and sitting right behind the target child, who has no idea who that person is. Sitting there, staring, thinking about what chance he might have in the parking lot as the child waits to be picked up. Or maybe the predator just follows the car home.

One prison study, the Butner Study, was conducted to determine if prisoners incarcerated for collecting abuse imagery were of little risk to actually touch a child. The study found these "collectors" were very likely to sexually abuse real children; a good number had actually done so and just not been caught.

As can be imagined, if this area of a child predator's life is messed up, so will other areas. Sometimes their relationships with other adults will be tenuous at best. In search of other sexual thrills, their interests branch out to bestiality, torture/rape, and other forms of sexual criminal behavior. If they live alone, most often their living areas are unkempt and unsanitary due to their preoccupation with their sexual addictions. Some places are so disgusting they require medical attention during the search warrant execution.

During one search warrant service, investigators had to go to a local home improvement store and purchase planks of plywood. These planks were laid over the garbage and feces covering the floor so the search team could walk unimpeded. During the suspect interview, the investigator placed a cold medicine rub across his upper lip to mask the overwhelming stench of the suspect. Investigators come back from warrants smelling of animal feces, garbage, and have to throw their clothes away at home. What's worse, some of these nasty places belonged to a suspect with more than an average amount of access to children—a coach, teacher, or youth pastor. The kids they worked with at their regular jobs were exposed to bacterial bombshells on clothing, footwear, hands, fingernails, or hair.

Please understand that these sexual predators do not care who they hurt or destroy in their wake. These one-person wrecking crews will stop at nothing in pursuit of their own sexual gratification from infants and toddlers on up—doing adult things, in an adult manner, with sick, incurable adults. There are online forums—some dark web, but most operating on widely used mainstream social media services—serving as discussion boards for child sexual abuse. Here are some actual comments seen on these forums.

"Such a pretty mouth."

"The tinier the hands, the bigger my c**k looks!"

"The only thing a daughter is good for."

Some are aroused by the child being in distress:

"I like it when they cry. Asking for their mother is a bonus."

"Lifeless eyes are the best!"

"I'm surprised he didn't break her with that."

This is the reason the search for child pornography and those dealing in it is so important. They're real-life monsters, plain and simple. Next, one of the most common methods child predators use to gain the trust, confidence, and esteem of potential victims is discussed: gifts.

To Recap:

- Predators can be anyone, even those invited into the stakeholder's life.
- Educators/predators are the ultimate chameleon of the predator class.
- School administrators need to be proactive and think ahead about educators/predators found on their campuses.

9

GIFTS AS A MEANS TO AN END

One of the most pervasive techniques used by child predators to groom a victim is by giving gifts. This is why children are taught to not accept candy from strangers. The digital age has changed not only the types of gifts but also the manner of delivery. Gift cards can be provided using online transactions easily missed by stakeholders. Cell phones can be ordered to alternate addresses. In one investigation, a predator sent several gifts to a vacant house and was finally caught when an observant and caring neighbor witnessed the deliveries and the child picking them up.

Gifts take innumerable forms as they are whatever is important to the child. Nicotine vapes, clothing, lingerie, bathing suits, food delivery, melatonin pills . . . anything can be provided with a relatively low chance of detection. If a stakeholder gets home from work hours after the child gets home from school, that's plenty of time to collect a gift package off the porch.

Predators do extensive research on how to provide a child with a phone and avoid stakeholder detection. These phones are doubly dangerous because the predators set up the phone. These phones can and often do contain spyware apps to further monitor the victims. The phone will be set up with a cloud account the suspect has access to, monitoring all traffic coming into and out of that device. The predator will have all the information needed to manipulate the child victim.

It's important to remember a smartphone does not need cellular service to operate as a phone. With a WiFi connection and one of any number of apps allowing the user to make phone calls and send text messages, there is no difference in the capabilities of a phone with cellular service and one that does not.

Modern GPS trackers add another layer of danger to grooming gifts. These trackers have become very small and extremely light; some are even smaller than a quarter. Even the smallest of dogs can carry one with ease on its collar, which is one of the legitimate uses of these devices: finding a lost dog. While some of these trackers need a direct connection with a host device in order to work, such as a networked SIM card, a large number of them do not. In fact, their signals can hitch a ride on nearby devices and networks to report their location that way.

Knowing the location of someone is part of the equation for a sexual predator. The other important piece of knowledge is how long a person will be where they are. Check-in options on social media have been around for a while, and now there are a litany of check-in applications available. There's no disputing the value in knowing where a loved one is, and that is a legitimate use for these check-ins. But kids developing their own friendship circles and sharing their locations isn't something that should go unchecked by a stakeholder. Teenagers go places often without direct parental supervision beyond a ride to the theater, funplex, or the mall. A child checks in at their destination, and the social media post fest begins, highlighting the memories of the outing. Going to destinations like these can last hours. What if the child has accepted a friend request from a social media profile they thought was a fellow teenager but was instead secretly an adult predator? Worse, a *local* predator who shows up? The child, distracted by the texting and posting, doesn't see the predator closing in until it's too late.

It's not necessary to discuss what catastrophes could unfold from that point forward.

A small hole can be cut into a stuffed animal and a tracking device inserted, lost in the stuffing unless specifically felt and searched for. There's a market catering to parents legitimately bugging their children—attractive bracelets and clip-ons for backpacks designed to house a tracking device—for legitimate reasons. But what happens when a predator gives one of these bracelets to a child? The child and stakeholder may not recognize this piece of jewelry for what it is. It's very wise for stakeholders to acquaint themselves with what these devices look like by searching "GPS bracelet" online.

Asset tracking—whether it's a car, forklift, or a person—is an industry worth billions of dollars annually. The cheapness, small size, and wide availability of these tracking devices just being one click away from purchase make them a very valid threat, and stakeholders need to be on the lookout for them.

Children make "wish lists" on shopping websites so friends can see what they'd like for a birthday or Christmas gift. But these lists are also a boon of information to a child predator. One item often high on these wish lists is a smartwatch. Big name smartwatches are expensive and out of reach for some folks. A secondary market of cheaper smartwatches compatible with popular operating systems is ever evolving. Several of these watches are specifically marketed as GPS trackers disguised as regular smartwatches. These GPS smartwatches can come with a networked SIM installed and still be paired normally with the child's phone. Thus, the device is constantly broadcasting location data as long as the predator pays the bill.

What does a stakeholder do to stay vigilant against this threat? As always, regular room inspections should be conducted. Look for pieces of jewelry or other accouterments not purchased by a stakeholder in the child's life. Look specifically for wrist-worn items that look like a watch but aren't. They will have a quarter or half-dollar-sized round object where the watch would be. Some of these have changeable decorative "faces" to further disguise what they are. Closely inspect other items the stakeholder doesn't recognize. There are Bluetooth speakers that are also spy cameras. Legitimately, they would be used as "nanny cams," but a naïve child could be persuaded to connect this device to their home network, thus enabling the predator to have twenty-four/seven access to what happens in that room. In one case, a fifteen-year-old girl was gifted a Bluetooth speaker from a boyfriend but it also had a spy camera, which not only captured her in unclothed situations, but her mother and her friends as well.

Using the technology against itself is a highly effective option in detecting unauthorized devices. Smartphones alert that an unknown device appears to be traveling with the user. Do not ignore these messages as flukes. While there may be a legitimate reason for the alert, like a passenger having a tracker on their keys or someone's dog at the dog park, it may be alerting you to a tracker unknowingly acquired by the child or even placed on the car itself. Investigate these alerts until they are explained. These alerts will guide the user to locate the device and also block that device from pairing with the alerting phone. There are a number of spy gadgets that can detect signals from hidden cameras and GPS devices. In addition to protecting children, these devices are handy for checking hidden surveillance in rental properties and hotel rooms. These devices vary in effectiveness and cost, and again should be used as snitches and not a catch-all for detecting unwanted surveillance.

An example follows: A stakeholder calls her child down for dinner. The child is wearing a really fashionable bracelet, and she asks her daughter where it came from. The child immediately becomes nervous and defensive, providing a vague excuse as to origins. The stakeholder takes the bracelet from the child and finds a small hatch on the backside of the quarter-sized medallion in the center of the bracelet. She opens it and out falls an obvious GPS tracker. The child continues to not provide any plausible answer. The child also appears very scared. The stakeholder should be very cognizant of the hard fact the child thought it was just a pretty bracelet from someone she'd met online and had been manipulated into thinking was a true and trusted friend. The child is now realizing just how vulnerable she made herself, replaying every interaction of the very secret online relationship. The stakeholder and child are two very scared people unsure of what to do next. But if the stakeholder has a plan for the discovery of untoward online behavior, it's time to put that plan into effect. Instead of pornography or sexually explicit conversations, the parent has discovered a different facet of the secret relationship, thus, the same plans should apply.

- Call the police for a report.
- Document and mitigate by collecting the child's devices and PIN codes/passwords. Remove the battery from the GPS device, if possible.
- Reassure and love the child. Be supportive and understanding, but firm of resolve.
- Cooperate with responding officers and follow-up detectives.

One of the goals a child predator has when gifting a phone is obtaining pictures of the victim. The next chapter focuses on the different types of information these pictures can provide, outside of the visible picture itself.

To Recap:

- Gifts are a powerful grooming tool.
- Check the child's room often for new jewelry and electronics.
- Investigate device alerts to detected tracking devices.

10

PICTURES ARE PRICELESS

A twenty-seven-year-old man was soliciting and obtaining nude images of teenage girls online. During the investigation, a printed image of three girls is found. They sat at a cheap veneer particle board folding table. In the background was a cinder block wall painted orange and white, part of what appeared to be a mascot painted on that same wall, like a horse's tail and hind legs, was found in the suspect's possession.

There were backpacks in front of them on the table, so it was pretty easy to deduce those girls were in a school environment.

The letters "AIRF" ran vertical on the block wall, cut off at the top and bottom. Using a super-secret law enforcement online search tool known as Google, one of the top words in the English language for letters in that order is Fairfield. Well, there was a Fairfield community in the area with a middle school, but the colors and mascot didn't match. With a Fairfield something or other in several states in the country, more information would be needed.

Or was there already enough information in the picture itself? Taking a second look, it was posted recently, and it was December. The weather for the last week was unseasonably warm, but these girls had big puffy jackets, mittens, and hats. It was cold. Using the posting date, the weather forecasts were checked to find out where it was really cold, and results settled in on the Northeast to the Midwest. A school district with a middle school with matching colors and a similar mascot, a Mustang, was located. That school district's police department was contacted and a copy of the picture sent.

A few minutes later, the girls were positively identified and the parents were notified. Using nothing but a picture and Google, and a little insider help, these girls were identified in under thirty minutes.

Seeing a picture for more than face value is an essential skill for an online child exploitation investigator. While there are specialized schools for photo clue analysis for law enforcement, most investigators hone this skill through reviewing what suspects did in order to gain access to a child.

A digital photo is not just an image. It's a data file which can and does contain quite a bit of "geek" information about the picture. Using a third-party application to view the EXIF (exchangeable image file format) data is a handy way to learn more about a photo. EXIF is data used by devices to handle pictures. In order to do this, the device needs to know certain information about a photo. EXIF data contains information on aperture, flash, and exposure settings.

Along with make and model, if the device has a user assigned name, such as Jeff's iPhone, it likely will transmit with the photo if sent from one device to another in, say, a text message. And if the location settings are turned on, the GPS data goes along with the photo. How is this applicable to a child's online life? The good news is that social networks scrub that data from photos posted to their services, so it's not available if someone downloads a photo from a social media site. But what about phone-to-phone communications?

For discussion's sake, a thirteen-year-old boy has an iPhone he named "Jeff's iPhone." He's trying to do the online safety things right. His gamer-tag, which he also uses in the chat boards of his favorite gaming app, doesn't contain his real name or any other identifiers. A few weeks ago, he met another gamer and they began chatting, moving those chats to each other's phone standard text messaging and, recently, phone calls. The other gamer asks for a selfie, which Jeff takes in his bedroom and sends via text messaging. What thirteen-year-old Jeff doesn't know is the other gamer is a preferential sex offender, and what Jeff doesn't understand is in sending that photo, he's given himself away. The sex offender has a third-party application which makes all that EXIF data readable. The sex offender knows Jeff's real first name and his exact location.

These third-party applications will even plot the GPS coordinates into a mapper, and thanks to Google Maps, this sex offender knows what street Jeff lives on, what his house looks like, and since that GPS is pretty accurate, now knows what part of Jeff's house his room is located. So it's not just a picture of Jeff.

It's everything.

To Recap:

- Background clues unwittingly allowed in pictures provide a treasure trove of information used to locate a child.
- A digital photo is not just a picture. It's a data file.
- A picture is everything.

II

BASIC TYPES OF CHILD ABUSE IMAGES AND OTHER USAGES OF SEXUAL IMAGES

There are essentially two kinds of child pornography. The first and most egregious type is what law enforcement calls crime scene photos, that is, photos or videos of a child being sexually abused. These are taken by the abuser in digital still images or videos. They may be of a child engaged in a sexual act with an adult, with other children at the direction of an adult abuser, or with themselves at the direction of the abuser. Investigators triage these cases immediately in order to locate, identify, and rescue the victims, plus arrest the perpetrators.

The second type of child pornography are those images taken voluntarily by subjects participating in sexual acts with other kids of similar age or by themselves. Investigators still assign an expedited status for these cases, but for a wholly different reason—to keep the images out of the hands of the child pornography collector.

Both these forms of child pornography are actively traded like baseball cards. There are even several well-known series of child pornography that feature chronological serial sexual abuse of a child. The abusers often tag the child with a pseudonym to identify the files in online conversations.

If the files are not traded by the accepted series name, they're traded by genre, age, sex, physical characteristics, and the acts involved, with filenames like "two twelve-year olds **** and ****." These "collectors" categorize and organize their collections like they would their income taxes by year or vacation pictures by location. They zip them up and send them electronically to others in exchange for files they don't have, particularly if the images fall into a genre they're interested in. Some collections are quite extensive and organized better than the Library of Congress.

Yet another category within pornographic images are those "leaked" by ex-boyfriends and ex-girlfriends. This category is "revenge porn." Much time is spent on these cases because the images are feeding the machine of depravity which can cause someone to seek out and abuse an innocent child. As parents and educators, consistent efforts need to be made to hammer home how illegal this behavior is. Tell them that those nude images are not funny, not cute, and not even erotic in a healthy way.

One attention-getting question to start a conversation with age-appropriate children is simply, "Would you come to school naked and go about your day?" The answer is no, followed by a chuckle at such an outrageous question, but in effect that's what they're doing when that image gets leaked out.

Do investigators like to get the person who's collecting child pornography? Absolutely. But that's not any child exploitation investigator's ultimate goal. Their ultimate goal is to find the person who's actually abusing a child and rescue that child. Once rescued, that child is no longer Jane or John Doe. They have a name, age, favorite color, and ice cream. Part of this type of investigation includes sending the case information to the National Center for Missing and Exploited Children. The purpose of this is because the center maintains a library to track the number and location of investigations yielding files of the identified victims.

This helps investigators track the trading of these images from offender to offender. In some cases, the images feature someone who is "age difficult," meaning the age of the child is difficult to determine without knowing who the child is and the age they were when the picture was taken.

The final category in the usage of pornographic images is a development out of revenge porn, and it is simply called extortion. A form of this extortion racket is explained in the next chapter, but it's a problem that frequently spills out of the home and into schools. It can be the result of a clandestine online exploitive relationship souring, or worse, it could have been the final goal of the suspect all along. Most often, when the child stops sending sexually explicit images, the suspect threatens to expose the child, or demands money to stop them from sending sexually explicit photos to the child's friends and stakeholders.

An emerging derivative of this type of extortion and revenge porn has to do with school politics. An example would be a high school student running for student council. At some point during the campaigning phase, sexually explicit images the student took in middle school emerge again in an effort to disrupt the voting and democratic process.

When these types of events happen, multiple student recipients are sent the images and are transmitted to others during the school day. The whispers get louder, or a student alerts a school tip line about the situation and school administration gets involved. First and foremost:

- Do not take pictures of the illicit photos.
- Do not email or transmit the images, and this includes in school computer systems.
- Do not delete any content whatsoever.

Do not store or otherwise maintain the images using a school district or, worse, a personally owned device in order to "collect evidence."

These mistakes, although with the best of intentions, happen all too frequently. In taking pictures of the images, child pornography is produced. Sending them in an email to school administration is technically distribution of child pornography. Storing the images is to possess them. The images, if emailed, are stored in the sender's and recipient's(s') email, and in any backup system in place. Simply deleting the images does not eradicate them, even if the trash is emptied. Deleting a file only removes the header of the file and keeps the operating system from showing it as available. It is still there, in the hard drive, intact, and recoverable. It would take a robust drive wipe to get rid of it entirely.

Instead, heed the familiar refrain of a police supervisor on their way to a major scene. They will tell their subordinates to hold what they've got, and keep the scene from getting any worse by their own actions. Secure the device(s) containing the evidence, and call law enforcement.

A child's images aren't just troublesome in school life. They often continue into adulthood, such as a twenty-something woman's boss receiving an email from a fake email address asking if he'd like to get to know his employee a little better. The email contains a picture of the woman taken when she was much younger. This was done by the suspect with no warning or demand of money to not send the images. The sole motive was to cause the woman pain and hardship.

Or perhaps a woman's fiancé gets an email from an anonymous source asking if the woman's new fiancé would like to see the attached pictures of questionable decisions made in her sexual past.

Another similar investigation traced emails back to a suspect in another state whom the female victim had never known. She also didn't know why he'd want to humiliate her with such graphic disclosures. A fellow investigator in that state was tapped for follow-up help. It turned out this stranger happened upon the complainant's pictures on an online photo-sharing website belonging to the woman's husband. He mistakenly left it publicly viewable after uploading the images she had sent him. The suspect socially engineered her and identified her for the express purpose of seeing a young, pretty, successful, and happy woman suffer.

The perceived anonymity of an online environment seems to override basic senses of civility. What people wouldn't say to another standing face to face is easily said in an online setting because there's no emotional consequence. It's the modern-day equivalent of punishment by stoning: picking up a rock, throwing it, and walking away.

It's a burden on stakeholders to warn children about these behaviors because of the laws of unintended consequences and so-called internet trolls who use information to cause pain in others for the sake of doing it. The permanency of digital information allows for old hurts to fester and grow, and the evidence to exist indefinitely, ready to be used again and again.

To Recap:

- Collections are like anything else someone values. Collectors collect.
- Do not save, transfer, send, or otherwise maintain copies of sexually explicit images.
- Pictures are forever.

(12)

ROMANCE AND HOOKUP SCAMS

In the previous chapter, the strategy of sexual extortion by predators was introduced. An emerging trend in this extortion racket is one beginning with the promise of love and companionship. Imagine a fourteen-year-old boy in his room alone receiving a friend request from a pretty girl, a girl he's never seen before. He accepts the request, and "she" sends a flirty message. The conversation turns sexual, and the girl proposes trading explicit photographs and videos. The boy sends a picture of his privates, expecting the girl to respond in kind. Instead, the conversation turns sinister: *Send me five hundred dollars or I'll show all your friends and family what you're really like.*

The child says, "I'm just a kid; I don't have five hundred dollars." A negotiation begins, and the boy sends what he can afford. But the demands keep coming because the child sent money without telling his parents. The "girl" sends screenshots of a message draft to the boy's mother with his nudes attached, threatening to send it to her. This overwhelms the boy, and he doesn't know what to do. If the stakeholder hasn't been following the advice of this book, making it clear the child can come to them with anything, likely the boy won't tell them until the burden becomes too much.

Investigators refer to this form of online exploitation as a "romance/hookup scam." These scammers use carefully constructed scripts to induce victims to place themselves in a compromising situation and get money from them. While adult men with money are the typical target, juveniles can get caught up in their snare too.

A few things to remember about these scams:

- Do not send money. This only leads to requests for more.
- Scam operators can and will expose their victims.
- Do not message the profile back after the money demands begin.

So how did the scammer find the child's profile to begin with? The most common way is the child was operating a publicly viewable social media profile. Looking at things a different way, a juvenile with a fully public profile actually puts his online friends in more danger of exploitation because he's making his friends easily discoverable by predators. It's very common for predators to victimize one person and then move through that victim's friends list doing the exact same thing.

The child may protest at keeping their profile private. But in this day and age, it is very easy for legitimate friends to find each other's social media profile. The easiest is for the child to just tell the potential online friend their username, but the app itself almost negates the need to do that. Modern social media algorithms work to keep their users engaged with the application. The app constantly tracks what users do and compares friend lists with other profiles they interact with. Ever wonder why the "suggested friends" on a social media profile is very spot on?

When teaching a male child about romance scams, it is helpful to present the psychosexual differences between men and women. Males see and respond to sexually explicit material in a much stronger way than women do. This can and will drown out common sense. Females as a general rule do not care to see a picture of a boy's penis right off the bat, if ever. Tell the male child that on the internet, the men are men and so are the women—a "female" stranger on the internet asking for a penis picture or to sext isn't a girl at all, as a general rule. Tell them to avoid interaction with the profile altogether.

As if all this isn't enough, some kids just can't handle the pressure of being exposed and actually harm themselves, up to and including suicide. Stories about these sad tragedies are all too common. Think about how unnerving it would be for an adult to fall for such a scam, and it's possible to imagine just how world-ending this experience would seem to a child. For this reason, if a child divulges to a stakeholder being involved in one of these romance scams, it should be treated the same as a teenager calling for a ride home after having too much fun at a party. A stakeholder cannot and should not get angry at the child for doing the right thing in asking for help, regardless of how many bad decisions were made prior.

In chapter 13, the photography discussion continues with another facet to consider in conjunction with social media: does the user actually own and control what they post online?

To Recap:

- Do not send money.
- Document and preserve evidence in this scam just as any other exploitive event discussed in this book.
- Report the incident to law enforcement.

13

INSTANT PHOTOGRAPHY

Back in the day, the closest thing to instant photography was a Polaroid. Point and aim, push a button, out comes a picture. If one didn't like the picture, it could be barbecued, shredded, set on fire, put in a fish fryer, whatever, it was gone. That was the only original. Children taking naked pictures of themselves isn't exactly a new thing; it was just not as easily shareable.

In the 1990s, a junior yearbook photographer took several nudes of herself and developed them in the school darkroom. Problem was, she left a sheet of negatives behind. Somebody found them, developing a hundred before plastering them in the boys' bathrooms all over the school. Not all of these were recovered, of course, but the point is, there was a known value of how many were out there.

Digital photography is copyable, manipulatable, and easily shareable. It's like going to a kid's birthday party, and afterwards all of the helium-filled balloons are taken outside and let go. One goes this way, another goes that way, one gets run over by a jet plane, and unless one can levitate, those balloons aren't coming back. That's digital photography in a nutshell.

A common complaint is "somebody did something with my pictures." If those pictures were freely given out to someone else, that action changes the nature of that picture. It is no longer that person's picture.

It becomes a picture of them.

The same holds true, albeit in a slightly different fashion and reason, for images posted on social networking. Yes, a person signs up for a social networking account and sets up what becomes known as "their account." They can direct others to "their page" for "their content." The simple fact needing understanding is that once posted, the content is no longer theirs. If one does not own the server space that content is on, it's not solely theirs any longer. Taking a look at the terms of service (TOS) for a few major social networks illustrates this point:

From Facebook's TOS:

Specifically, when you share, post, or upload content that is covered by intellectual property rights on or in connection with our Products, you grant us a non-exclusive, transferable, sub-licensable, royalty-free, and worldwide license to host, use, distribute, modify, run, copy, publicly perform or display, translate, and create derivative works of your content.

From Twitter's TOS:

This license authorizes us to make your Content available to the rest of the world and to let others do the same. You agree that this license includes the right for Twitter to provide, promote, and improve the Services and to make Content submitted to or through the Services available to other companies, organizations or individuals for the syndication, broadcast, distribution, Retweet, promotion or publication of such Content on other media and services, subject to our terms and conditions for such Content use.

From Snapchat's TOS:

To the extent it's necessary, when you appear in, create, upload, post, or send Public Content, you also grant Snap Inc., our affiliates, and our business partners the unrestricted, worldwide, perpetual right and license to use your name, likeness, and voice, including in connection with commercial or sponsored content.

While nearly all of the major social networks' TOS state the individual account holders still maintain ownership of their content, they are in all reality co-owners of that content with that social network. What's more, these same social networks also very clearly state that by posting content, they are in fact splitting ownership of that content with other users as they share, repost, or retweet a user's content. And if that user's account is publicly viewable by anyone, they can and will use that content in numerous forms because it's in the public domain, right where the original user placed it.

Referring back to Merriam-Webster's definition of share from the introduction, another facet of the definition includes to *post something on a social media platform*. It provides an example sentence: "Fans were also quick to screenshot and share the photo." Anybody who's ever screenshotted or right-clicked and saved a photograph from the internet or social media rightfully feels a sense of ownership over that item publicly shared on a social media platform. And from that sense of ownership comes entitlement to use it as they see fit.

Here's a case study to illustrate this point. Before going further, it's necessary to introduce a term called "tribute." There are music groups called tribute bands who pay homage to a more famous band by playing their music and imitating their style, dress, and mannerisms. They go by the adage of imitation being a sincere form of flattery. Typically, a tribute means to show respect or affection by most scholarly definitions.

There is another form of tribute which fits into an already identified paraphilia. It's called salirophilia. This is the sexual fetish/desire to desecrate or degrade an object representative of a person's sexual attraction. Most often the desecration and degradation inflicted on that object is a sexual act. It should not come to anyone's surprise that there are websites dedicated to this activity, and the most commonly degraded object online is a photograph.

That being said, a young adult woman complained to law enforcement that pictures from her social media had been posted on this type of tribute website. Other users had printed out those pictures, performed a sexual act to them, and videotaped or taken pictures of that act. They then posted those images and videos on the site. There were a whole host of disgusting comments as well.

The woman who made the complaint indicated her social media profiles were wide open, publicly accessible, and viewable by anyone, and these tributed photos were pulled from her profiles. Laws condemning this activity vary widely, from a chargeable offense to no violation of law found. The age of the subject in the photo may come into consideration, but the simple reason complicating things is the photos were freely accessible to anyone, and as such, there is minimal expectation of control over what people do with what's shared.

Sharing means with anyone, including these nefarious types, even if the original intent was anything but that. So with a good grasp of what one is up against, it's time to turn attention to developing plans to deal with it all.

To Recap:

- There is no known value of image copies once an image is posted online.
- Posting content on social media gives co-ownership of that content to the social network.
- People can, and will, do anything they want with images on social media, and most of it isn't illegal.

(14)

IS THERE A PLAN?

It's time to circle back to the third question: *Is there a good plan to deal with what's discovered?*

Here are the recommended steps and the rationale behind them.

It's very common for online predation to be advanced before it is detected by stakeholders. That's because the technology and methods used change quickly, many times within a few days. Taking up a child's device for one week will show that the scope is clear. Five days later, there's inappropriate or illegal content. Stakeholders have to be vigilant on a routine basis.

The mere action of physically inspecting a child's device does more to prevent online misbehavior and detects more predation than any parental software on the market. This is not to say parental apps are worthless. There are several good ones out there, but think of them as a good snitch. And there's that time-honored adage in law enforcement that there's nothing like a good snitch to detect and solve crime. Parental control apps are the snitches. Between taking up the devices and deploying parenting apps, the child will know that each action on the device is subject to interpretation and detection. Then, they will govern behavior on the device.

Perhaps more importantly, in explaining why the device is being taken up, the child will probably feel more comfortable talking about something uncomfortable happening in an online environment. Part of this conversation is emphasizing improper solicitation isn't their fault, even if the child did something out of naivety or silliness.

In establishing an ongoing dialogue, the child gets an extra feeling of comfort and security because they clearly know the stakeholder's expectations and their duty as a child to meet those expectations.

- The parent should buy the same device the child has. By doing so, the parent is already familiar with the basic layout and functions. Inconsistencies are more easily spotted than if the parent has an Android and the child an iPhone. If the camera roll or gallery applications are not where they should be, or not visible at all, they may have been moved to a more secure spot.

  Go into the applications listing of the device and look at the installed applications and navigate to them this way. Be familiar with "photo vault"–type applications, also commonly referred to as the "fake calculator." Some secret applications are designed to look and function like calculators until a passphrase is typed into the number pad, at which point the contents of the hidden applications are available for view.

  Check the internet browsing history for pornographic websites or questionable search patterns. Look closer at the history and see if large chunks of web searches and sites are missing. For example, if frequent web browser usage several times a day is the pattern and then suddenly two days are missing out of the history, that indicates deletion of certain articles. Children know a blank web history is a red flag of warning to parents, so they'll selectively delete items hoping it's not noticed.

  Check the camera roll or gallery applications for large swaths of missing pictures. If the child has certain applications with your permission, such as Snapchat, Instagram, Facebook, and so on, and these applications are found in a logged-off status, that's a point of concern. These applications are made to run in the background and provide notifications of new content. Logging them off can be an attempt to hide content.

  The child should be made to provide all passwords to applications not logged in at the time of your inspection.

  The goal is detection of a "managed phone." It's not uncommon for law enforcement to perform a forensic examination of a device and find upward of fifteen thousand text messages, some twenty thousand web history entries, thousands of lines of chat logs, and thirty thousand pictures and videos. A child doing what they should be doing with their devices has the same characteristics as far as content is concerned with a child unconcerned with parent interference.

They motor along without a care in the world, much like driving on the interstate following the speed limit—no fear or expectation of being pulled over, and they'd gladly fill up a phone's memory and ask for more. A child trying to conceal something will "manage" their phone, deleting content along the way, and if done in the right manner, can give the appearance there's nothing going on with the phone. The seeming absence of activity should be just as alarming as the discovery of offending content.

- This sounds very crude, but run text string searches on the search function of the device for slang terms for sex and body parts. What follows is an incomplete list of impolite words, apologies in advance: ass, butt, cock, cum, dick, fuck, ho, lick, penis, pecker, pole, rim, suck, tits, titty fuck, etc. Searches like these will highlight offending content no matter where it's hidden on the device, in most circumstances.

- Keep abreast of current available applications. If you find an application on your child's device you don't know, Google it. The search term "Parent tips for <insert app name here>" will have a list of talking points and safety concerns for each application. However, a good rule of thumb regarding any application would be to remove any followers the child or stakeholder doesn't know.

- Enable the private account feature or equivalent. Remove or disable the geotagging map feature that can pinpoint the location of pictures taken.

- Go back into the camera roll or gallery and review it for time stamp activity. Take a closer look at that seemingly harmless selfie. What time was it taken? An innocuous looking photo taken at 3:30 a.m. takes on a little more urgency. Why was the child awake? Who were they talking to?

- In the contacts section, look at each entry carefully. Look for recent call or text activity to a phone number not identified by name in the contacts.

Review slang names in contacts and ask the child to give you a real person's identity for each name. Look carefully at any emojis used to denote a contact. Get educated on emojis commonly used to denote sexual activity, such as an eggplant, which is a commonly used emoji to describe a penis, or a peach, which is used to denote a vagina. There's also a rocket used in conjunction with a subway train in a tunnel to represent sexual intercourse. A set of boggled out eyes and a swimsuit emoji indicates a peep show of sorts (sexting photos). Several different types of open-mouthed smiley faces in a row suggests oral sex, as they simulate mouth movements around a penis.

Several extended fingers preceding an "okay" finger gesture, followed by water droplets indicates manual stimulation of the vagina. A fist emoji in front of an eggplant, followed by water droplets and a smiley face, indicates a desire for manual masturbation of the penis with ejaculation on the face. A shower head, eggplant, and a peach denote sex in the shower. Basically, anything with an eggplant emoji is highly suspect.

- It's time to move on to the internet router. The router is the device routing all traffic coming through your internet to the device requesting it. Make a list of all devices that should be seen on the router. These will include all phones, tablets, school-issued laptops and devices, desktops, smart television, and so on. What's important here is when the router/network is "interrogated," or quizzed for what is connected to it, the list should only contain devices the stakeholder knows about and consented to be there. For those readers looking to stretch their "computer geek legs," what follows is a go-to for router interrogations using traditional network forensic techniques. Afterward, there will be a discussion on using freely available applications available for download on a smartphone or other device.

Parents need to know the IP address of the router on the home network. In many instances, the next step is what's called an IPconfig in a command prompt window. Under the heading Default Gateway in the WiFi settings, there will be an IP address. Copy down that address and then open an internet browser window and type in that address, then hit enter. The next prompt is the router name and password. There will then be a bunch of information displayed, but what's important is the list of devices currently connected to and past connections to it.

There are a number of applications designed to this process easily by performing the interrogation task on any network the app is connected to. Most, if not all, network providers like AT&T and Comcast offer applications for download that monitor several aspects of your home network, including what's on it.

Either way it's accomplished, pull out the list of devices that should be connected to the router and identify them in the router's list. Any devices not on the list are suspect devices needing to be accounted for. For example, if the approved devices list includes the parent's phones, the kids' phones, a couple of iPads, the smart television, and a desktop, but there is also an Android when everybody in the house uses Apple, that is the device that needs to be asked about and found.

Hidden devices are a problem because there's a good chance these devices were provided to the child by the abuser in order to escape parental authority and discovery. These devices can be mailed and delivered by Amazon or sent to a third-party retailer for pickup. Most often the device is a cell phone, but it could be a tablet or even a small laptop. And the device doesn't even have to have any kind of paid service to work. Any WiFi connection will do just fine. Remember, a WiFi connection and any freely available third-party text and calling application is all that's needed to carry on a clandestine exploitive relationship with the child.

Another source of hidden devices is the household itself. Sometimes a parent will have kept a device long enough that it's paid for. Then, when a new device is purchased, the old one comes home in a box and tossed in a junk drawer or on a top closet shelf, forgotten until the child finds it and puts it to use.

It's generally not a good idea to keep old devices lying around, and not just for this reason. If the house is burglarized, there's a good chance the old devices will get stolen. Since they still contain personal information, like bank accounts and private family information, they could be used to commit identity theft or to wipe out a bank account. These devices should be factory reset, which effectively wipes the device of any usable data. If the device contains a removable micro SD card, the card should be removed and reformatted. Lastly, be aware that children buy and sell devices to each other at school, which is another source of hidden devices.

Get creative in the search for hidden devices because they can be anywhere due to varying sizes.

Consider the size of a micro SD card: It's about half the size of a postage stamp. They and other small media-like flash drives have been found taped under bed rails, behind light switch plates, to the tops of ceiling fan blades, in picture frames, and even in waterproof containers in the toilet tank.

Here are a few tips for making the child a less attractive target during an inspection of social media accounts.

- Make the child's account a friend or follow a family member/friend who's in law enforcement, and it's obvious on their social media. If there's no one like that in the parent's circles, follow every single area law enforcement agency's social media accounts.

- Unfollow and block any account the child can't say how they know that person. Just as LinkedIn identifies first-, second-, and third-degree association indicators for their users, children will have these too (opponents from other sports teams, friends of friends, etc.). Parents should use discretion in allowing how many degrees of association are acceptable.
- Stakeholders should friend or follow the child's accounts.

Just as important as the steps *to do* to keep the child safer is what *not to do*. Both these components are essential.

If the worst fears are realized during a routine check of the child's device, it's discovered the child's sexting with someone in the same age group. Or there's a hidden device taped to the underside of a desk in the child's room containing images or texts of a clandestine exploitive relationship with an adult.

First, *do not explode* emotionally. This is not the same thing as a curfew violation or a car accident caused by recklessness. Yes, the child has done and said things they shouldn't. Maybe they have even photographed some body parts that no one should be photographing. These are things the child was taught not to do, but they did it anyway.

The child is a victim, plain and simple. If the predator is an adult, they broke their bond with society to protect and nurture children. Remember, the ultimate fault lies with the adult. The child wouldn't have done what they did if it hadn't been for that person. If the child wore grandpa's wristwatch in public and some crook put a gun in their face and stole it, the thief stole it through actions of their own. Yes, in a perfect world the child should be able to wear the heirloom without a care in the world. But in this case, a predator stole the child's innocence through conscious, illegal actions.

The reason why stakeholder reaction is so important is because the stakeholder is the closest ally the child has, even if that relationship hasn't been all that great lately. And if the exploitive relationship has deteriorated into threats of online exposure or blackmail, the child literally has nobody on their side. An explosive, yelling parent is counterproductive because the child knows they have made wrong decisions; yelling isn't going to make them see clearer what they already know.

Also, the first step in repairing the child's psychological damage is the stakeholder's initial reaction. The child will need a huge support system in the weeks and months, perhaps years, to come, and the stakeholder is a vital part of that healing network.

Lastly, law enforcement is going to need the child's willing cooperation, which includes a full forensic interview during which explicit details will be revealed. At the beginning of one of those interviews, if the child is old enough to understand, it will be explained that their parents will be notified of the contents of such an interview. Police investigators don't want a child holding back details they are afraid to reveal because of what parents will think. It will only delay or even hinder the investigation and goal of apprehension.

And always remember, the child isn't the only one their abuser is talking to. As the relationship has been discovered, the child obviously isn't available online so the suspect is likely paying attention to another victim. From an outward view, somebody else's child is getting the same treatment. Since these people often find victims through another victim's contact lists, that next child victim may be somebody the stakeholder already knows.

Second, resist every urge to communicate with the suspect. This includes directing anger at them, telling them to leave your child alone, threatening them, and so on. Above all, do not communicate with the suspect pretending to be the child. Many parents' first inclination might be to try and make the case stronger by continuing to allow the suspect to commit further crimes. Even in the most basic, undeveloped online relationship resulting in the child producing sexually explicit images, the elements of the offense are already there:

- Communicating in a sexually explicit manner with a person known to be a child
- Providing sexually explicit material to a person known to be a child
- Soliciting sexual imagery from a person known to be a child

If these elements are present, the case is already solid enough. Parents don't need to talk to this person and subject themselves to additional traumatic stress. It won't be too long before the suspect knows it's not the child texting or typing any more, especially if the relationship has been going on for a while. For instance, certain turns of phrase or grammatically correct sentence structure will tip the suspect off. These suspects also introduce secret codes or words in correspondence with their victims as periodic tests to ensure the child is still the one operating the device.

It's not uncommon for parents to discover a relationship between their child and an adult at a time when they were planning to meet for sex for the first time. Instead of calling the police, sometimes they take over the chats and meet the suspect themselves. The suspect arrives, and the parents confront them. The suspect assaults both parents in an effort to get away, and sometimes serious injuries are the result. Even during the controlled circumstances of a law enforcement undercover chat operation, these suspects frequently assault *armed and professionally trained* law enforcement officers. They arrive with knives, guns, and handcuffs, equipped with duct tape and gag materials.

Earlier in this book, there was a discussion about an airline pilot using his airline benefits to fly for free to meet a twelve-year-old boy he met on MySpace. This relationship was discovered by a teacher who observed the boy using his Blackberry to text in the middle of an exam. She took the phone and on her way back to the desk, read some of the messages. She alerted law enforcement, and this author's unit became involved. A review of the text messages discovered the plans to meet. Law enforcement took over the chats, with the boy assisting with how he spelled words and the inside details of their online relationship.

When the day his flight arrived, there were undercover officers in the terminal to observe him getting off the plane and picking up his rental car; they followed him from the airport to a hotel close to the boy's neighborhood. The premise of their meeting was that the parents were going to a dinner party and were leaving him alone for a few hours—that's why the boy and the suspect chose that day for him to come from Minnesota.

The undercover officers followed him from the hotel, and there were takedown units on the boy's street who knew the suspect's every move. When he parked in front of the boy's house, these units pulled him from the rental car as he urinated in his pants.

This intervention was possible because the boy's parents kept themselves out of the equation, resulting in a much more satisfying outcome: watching the suspect get swarmed, handcuffed, and arrested. Later, they were in court when the suspect got a seven-year prison sentence. If stakeholders are wanting to build a stronger case, they can do so by being a good witness.

Every criminal investigation begins with the simple tenant of preserving evidence until it is collected, no matter what kind of crime is under consideration. Consider a picture puzzle. It begins life as a picture of whatever, printed on cardboard. It is one whole piece at that point, before it is cut into a multitude of smaller pieces and put into a box before being shaken up and sealed, ready for purchase and amusement. Ever put together a puzzle and have one piece turn up missing? After looking under the table, then around the immediate area, there's still no missing piece. A criminal investigation is the same way. If the crime is a house burglary, the puzzle picture would be a snapshot of the home intact, the way it was left by the burglars.

Then somebody kicks in the back door, takes belongings, and leaves the scene to be discovered by the homeowner. When the investigator gets there, they find puzzle pieces much like opening a picture puzzle, and it's their job to put it together. When a crucial piece is missing, the investigator will begin by eliminating the obvious, their version of looking under your table and around the room. But how far can the investigator possibly go and what could have happened to it is often outside of their control; it may be gone forever.

Much like the missing puzzle piece, it got vacuumed up. The dog ate it. It fell out of the box at the factory or some jokester worker removed one piece from each puzzle he handled that day just to tick somebody off. And if that piece is gone forever, the puzzle will never be complete, just as a criminal investigation may stall because of evidence that's gone forever.

Which brings up the second most common reaction besides emotional explosions: destruction of the device. A lesser but still very consequential reaction is deleting the offending application or text messages. People ask all the time if this or that can be recovered after deletion, and the catch all answer given is "maybe," because it's true. It's dependent upon the device's operating system, available memory, and how the data was stored. Consumers demand their devices do an ever-increasing amount of tasks with limited amounts of memory and speed, so something invariably has to give, and that's usually memory space the user has elected to delete. The device could even be programmed to permanently get rid of items the user has deemed not needed.

Data in these cases is so crucial because it is an inanimate object, and thus, its intrinsic nature is that it cannot lie or otherwise misrepresent itself. Complainants, witnesses, and victims have trouble recalling details and suspects lie to save themselves, but the data is what it is. It either supports a conclusion or it does not. And if it's not available at all, forget it.

Upon discovery or confiscation of a cell phone or tablet, it becomes an evidentiary device, and the first rule of criminal investigations is to preserve evidence. The following is a list of steps to help preserve that evidence.

- Obtain the pass codes to the device if possible; write them down and tape them on the back of the device.
- Put the device in airplane mode and turn off the WiFi function on the device. These two actions remove the device from a network

environment and help preserve the data by negating the possibility of a remote wiping request.

- Many social networks allow for the screen name of an account to be changed by the user. Copy down any suspect screen names, along with the screen names of the child's account(s) and the dates they were observed.
- Make notes of what was seen because the police will ask about it later. Make notes as to what the child says, which may not be much at all. Try not to ask conclusion questions, which are inquiries whose answers depend upon things the child probably doesn't know.

Here's a rule of thumb that will help: mitigate circumstances. Make the most important decisions first so that additional damage cannot be done to the child or family. Police incident management's first rule is to keep the scene from getting worse. This could be evacuating people near a house fire or keeping traffic moving around a major accident. In other words, doing the right things at the right time in order to contain what's already happened.

Now it's time to walk through what will happen when a police officer responds after the illegal activity is discovered or there's a strong suspicion of illegal activity. And please, do call the police. Career criminals are deadly serious about continuing their crimes and will do so until put in jail.

To Recap:

- Parenting apps should be used as a tool, not a substitute, for stakeholder involvement.
- The stakeholder should buy a device they are already familiar with for the child.
- Preserving evidence is the first rule. Do not emotionally explode.

15

WHICH DEVICE SHOULD I BUY?

In 2008, the curriculum guide for internet safety presentations to children included the prompt to ask who had a cell phone. Having one used to be the exception to the rule. Safety recommendations have changed with technology. At one time, the safest option for children was a basic flip phone—no internet, no apps, just calls and texts. Smartphones were recommended with age, maturity, and demonstration of trust with the first device.

New applications and design with child safety in mind muddy the waters a little bit. Family cloud accounts and screen time controls across all devices give stakeholders the ability to see what children are doing. Several good third-party location applications give stakeholders the ability to see children's location in real time. For those with children of driving age, these applications even track driving habits—sudden accelerations, hard braking, and cell phone use are all reportable parameters.

With all these positive aspects to smartphones, there's definite advantages to those over the flip phones that used to be investigators' solid recommendations. So when it comes to which device to purchase, there's a third set of circumstances to consider to help a child be smarter, and therefore safer, using it.

As stated, things easily obtained tend to be cheaper intrinsically to their owners. It's accurate to say a child behaves better with technology if it's harder for them to obtain and they must wait longer for it than their peers. Even if it's just a few weeks after the child begins asking for or really needing one. In that interim, stakeholders can begin explaining expectations and consequences for abuse of the *privilege* of a stakeholder *lending* the child a smartphone. That's right, the child needs to understand they are not being given a smartphone and it belongs to the stakeholder. If a child knows what's expected of them and is invested in the process, then compliance to the rules, whether it's a phone, bike, skateboard, or car, is more easily obtained.

The easiest way to explain this process is a lesson in integrity. Perhaps at no time, other than the present, has integrity—doing the right thing when nobody's watching—been more important. Remember the majority of kids' online time is spent when stakeholders aren't watching their every move. Always remind them whose phone it is: the parents.

> To Recap:
>
> - Recommendations for which device to give to children will change with the evolution of technology.
> - Family cloud accounts, screen time controls, and third-party applications have made smartphones safer for children.
> - Smartphones are lent, not given, to children.

16

WHAT TO EXPECT FROM LAW ENFORCEMENT

Many people don't like calling the police to their homes. After all, police have their own jargon, their own ways of interacting with people, and the criminal justice system they've navigated daily and nightly for years is difficult for civilians to understand. Adding to it is the inevitable questions from the neighbors—Is everything okay? *Translation: I'm nosy and really want to know what kind of disaster has befallen your family.*

Given all these realities, don't think about the problem overnight or at work the next day. This may allow a criminal to destroy evidence, or worse, the child could do the same thing, out of some misplaced "loyalty" to the suspect. The reason this happens is the child has told the predator the jig is up. This brings the predator into damage control mode. They will do anything to keep from getting into trouble, and that includes ratcheting the psychological manipulations into overdrive, leaving the child in a mental "limp" mode, much like the check engine light on a car dashboard.

Typically, the officer or patrol deputy will arrive and ask what's going on. They have already been told by the dispatcher what was said on the telephone, but they will want to hear it again (and with more details).

The advice in the previous chapters about not losing temper bears repeating. The officer arriving and sitting at the kitchen table invites emotions never before invoked, even when the offense was detected. Because this is where the rubber meets the road. If it wasn't real before, it is now. Anger at the child, the ex-spouse who bought the phone, the child's friend for introducing the suspect to the child, and so on, is now boiling over because of the questions being asked. Anger doesn't help the situation. If the child sees the parent displaying these characteristics, then they will probably act the same way with the police officer. And, as has been stressed already, an investigation with the child's cooperation will go much more smoothly than one without.

The responding officer or deputy may be technologically adept, or not. Regardless, their job is to obtain the who, what, where, why, and how of the case. In the case of online exploitation, do not expect the patrol unit to record every nook and cranny of concerns and problems. Their job is to obtain enough information and evidence to indicate a crime has occurred and give the detectives something to work with until they contact for more information.

Patrol officers are like good handymen—they know a good amount about a lot of things, just not everything about every single type of case. The "good news" is that the problem of online exploitation is a common one. Patrol officers have received training on this type of case and have investigated them before, so they'll probably collect a good amount of information. Don't forget the list of devices, user names, and passwords for the child's devices and accounts. The officer will need to see this list. It's a good idea to have a copy on hand, as the reporting systems of today have the capability of scanning documents into the case, rather than the officer having to reproduce them in the text part of the report.

Once the report is taken by the patrol officer, it's referred to a specialized detective through established procedures for that police agency. From there, the case is triaged based on certain factors, for level of severity and importance.

Here are commonly used assessment factors:

- How are the victim and suspect related—do they know each other in real life? Is the victim a child and suspect adult, and not kid on kid?
- Has sexual contact already occurred?
- Is there a high likelihood of the victim's endangerment?
- If the child and the criminal haven't met yet, is a meeting planned or imminent?
- What is the age of the victim? Generally, the younger the victim, the more exigent the circumstances.

In much the same way that a broken toe is placed behind a stabbing in an emergency room, two age-appropriate teenagers sexting each other will score below an online exploitive relationship between a kid and a middle-aged adult about to get on a plane to pick up the child and take them to a motel for sex.

This is not to diminish the importance of each case and child. As common as the problem is to police, they do understand this is probably the first time it's happened to each particular stakeholder.

Here's something to help understand the child exploitation investigator. This type of investigator is experienced and well trained. One does not hire into this position. The average length of police service for a new child exploitation investigator is between eight and ten years. These are the type of police officers who've been in fights, car chases, and life and death situations.

They're calm and collected: seasoned fact-finders with a proven track record for results. In their current job as child exploitation investigators, they've seen things most of their coworkers in other policing divisions can't picture. Heartache, disgust, numbness, and intolerance for the pain are just some of the understandable side effects of the work they do. It takes a special kind of person to witness unspeakable acts committed against our most vulnerable and come to work every day.

They take a personal vow they will do all that can be done legally to return safety and security to all child victims. They do these things because there is no greater feeling in a law enforcement career than to rescue a child who could never help themselves, who may not ever have been believed. To watch the fire of hope rekindled in the eyes of a child is to see the dead come to life again.

These cops can't drive more than ten minutes through their city without seeing someplace they've been in pursuit of predators. A luxury high-rise along the freeway where an offshore oil-rig boat captain lived while sexually assaulting a friend's daughter. A neighborhood with a sixteen-year-old with a collection of infant child pornography, and a no-tell motel where a child pimp used to ply his trade.

Patience is encouraged when apparent disinterest from the assigned investigator through occurrences such as a lack of timely returned phone calls happens. Please know the case is in the best possible hands and there's always another case that's worse. Good cops will never promise the world, only their best efforts.

These types of investigations run long, outside of life-or-death emergencies, because the subpoenas and search warrants needed have an average response time rate of between thirty to forty-five days. The major social networks can receive thousands of legal processes a day. They too must prioritize their responses, based on their list of assessment factors.

That being said, most cases require multiple legal processes (subpoenas and search warrants) to establish the location of a possible suspect—one to the social network for the data, one to the ISP (Comcast, AT&T, etc.), so that's an average of sixty days just to find out minimal information on a suspect. A large caseload doesn't bother an exploitation investigator, like it does a homicide or burglary investigator, because there's only so much can be done at one time with one of these cases—send a subpoena, wait, send another, wait.

Granted, exigent circumstances will speed up the timeline greatly. The ISPs don't agree among themselves about much, but child exploitation is the exception to the rule. Even criminal hackers have been known to cooperate with law enforcement investigations because of the severity of the issue. Examples of exigent circumstances are immediate plans to meet, missing victims, a sexual assault that just happened, or any other circumstance which would lead a person to believe loss of life or physical danger is a real possibility. Outside of those, these investigations do take time.

Earlier in this text, the idea was introduced regarding the needed support network for victims as they recover from the exploitation. Trusted relatives are a great addition for immediate parent support, but do not forget about the large amount of time the child spends elsewhere, especially their school.

In this age of instant communication with educators, it's not uncommon to have several lines of active communication with the child's teachers about grades, projects, even band concerts. Even if previous emails have been a little adversarial, perhaps a disagreement over a disciplinary event, teachers got into their line of work because they truly care about children. When children thrive in their educational environment, it's a huge source of pride.

When tragedy strikes a student's family, the teachers often hear of it and grieve with the child, either openly or to themselves. When children are killed in accidents, that empty desk looms larger than life. If that teacher catches a particular child looking at that desk in a longing manner, they'll call the counselor and have that student brought into the office. They attend funerals, set up dinner chains, even lead fundraisers, depending upon the relationship between the teacher and child.

If a stakeholder knows a child has a healthy albeit deeper connection with a particular teacher, it would be a good move to add that teacher to the child's expanding support network. Bear in mind this action is closely regulated by school rules, but that teacher would surely do all they could do to help.

Notification to school officials should be considered for another very important reason. In cases of children who've interacted with multiple predators online, they lose track of who they told what. In cases where the main predator is under investigation and/or already arrested, it doesn't mean that child isn't in danger from someone else. It could be another predator has been silently digesting information, figured out where that child is and goes to school, and is planning some sort of surprise interaction. Schools are always on the lookout for danger, but knowing timely information is key in their proactive stance.

During the investigation, be encouraged to call or email the investigator with any updates affecting the assigned priority level. These would be gifts being mailed to the home, the child using a secret device missed the first time, or going out of their way to communicate with the suspect. Behavioral changes in children may need further investigation.

There always have been and always will be people who prey on children, so the only effective method to combat this problem is to eliminate or radically reduce the pool of available victims. But what happens after the crime is committed? In chapter 17, it's time to discuss getting victims and stakeholders the help they need to recover.

To Recap:

- If a predatory relationship is discovered, do not waste precious time thinking about calling law enforcement. It nearly always leads to destruction of vital evidence.
- This is a common call for service with law enforcement. Be ready with your evidence and information gathering discussed in these chapters.
- Depending on the circumstances, consider notifying the child's school, especially if there is a safety concern in that environment.

17

POST-VICTIMIZATION RECOVERY

The child is commonly referred to as the victim in an online exploitation crime, but the truth is that victimhood extends to the child's parents and siblings, along with other stakeholders. This is because a child victim isn't capable or in some cases legally able to defend and take care of themselves. As a consequence, the concept of secondary victimization applies to more than the primary child victim.

Secondary victimization refers to a continuing negative attitude encountered by victims after the crime is committed, sometimes referred to as "victim-blaming." Unfortunately, this negative attitude can come from within the criminal justice system itself.[1] While expected from the suspect's defense attorney or witnesses on their behalf, it can also come from prosecutors and judges. Perhaps the biggest source of secondary victimization is the judgment of peers. For parents it could be other parents or adults with condescending and judgmental looks.

> *How'd they let that happen under their noses?*
> *I'd never let that happen to my kid.*

When a child is victimized by an online predator, word travels fast among friends and classmates.

> *That's the girl who ran off with a forty-year-old pervert.*
> *That's the boy that the coach got a hold of.*

For others to treat victims this way distracts from the hard fact that the situation could just as easily be reversed. Parents should be well aware of how close they are every day to complete and total disaster. Deep down, children should know if online sexual predation can happen to someone they know, it can happen to anyone, including themselves.

Secondary victimization is one of the biggest impediments to mental health recovery from an online child exploitation event. Mental health as a concept has undergone an image rehabilitation lately, taking on more palatable names such as "self-care" and "personal awareness." This book argues this change in terminology is reflective of societal acceptance that this technological life humans have created is painful and toxic. To paraphrase the late comedian George Carlin, this change in nomenclature of various mental health issues is a generational watering down of the true nature of the human nervous system. The brain can only take so much destruction before it seeks a permanent vacation. Carlin goes so far to suggest that if the term "shell shock" was still in use, perhaps military veterans would have got the treatment they needed a long time ago.

Media technology enables access to the gruesomeness of life, whether it's combat, terrorist attacks, murderous shooting sprees, or child exploitation, all recorded or even live streamed for anyone with an internet connection. One doesn't have to be an actual victim of child exploitation to suffer another type of emotional processing disorder, that of the moral injury.

A moral injury is a strong cognitive and emotional response occurring after experiencing events that violate a person's moral or ethical codes. These events threaten deeply held beliefs and trust in societal norms required for the whole system to function.[2]

Online child exploitation definitely falls into this category and those susceptible to moral injury and/or post-traumatic stress include all stakeholders: parents, guardians, teachers, and those investigators and legal professionals charged with bringing these criminals to justice. As this second edition is being written, a well-known social media platform reported millions of users' login information was compromised via a malicious third-party application. Child pornographers obtained some of this user information and took over innocent people's accounts, in effect locking these users out. What happened next is truly horrible: these suspects uploaded child exploitative imagery to those compromised accounts which was viewed by their followers as a status update. Luckily, that social media platform's internal processes caught the imagery very quickly which resulted in those affected profiles being taken down in short order. But the damage was done. People who would ordinarily never see those horrific images were exposed.

What also must not be forgotten is the moral injury and post-traumatic stress inflicted on children exposed to exploitative material. A common scenario that a child can unwittingly come into contact with exploitative material involves the online gaming community. A user group is formed within an online game and a new, unknown user joins. Out of the blue, with no warning whatsoever, this new user uploads graphic child exploitation imagery and disappears. The child is left there sitting there on their couch, controller in hand, mouth open in shock at what just happened, this unwanted realization children their age and much younger are subjected to varying degrees of rape and exploitation. Do they tell their parents? The answer to that question very well depends upon following the guidance in this book, which relates to how much the child fears losing their digital freedoms.

Exposure to child exploitation imagery in the course of mitigating their own child's victimization destroys stakeholders' foundational belief that children are supposed to be the ultimate protected class. This is also an example of moral injury and is made worse by the feelings of parental failure at protecting their own child. If left unchecked, it's very easy for a stakeholder to stay stuck at that stage of self-blame and not recognize the value of their own actions.

They can't see the heroic actions they took after their own child was victimized:

- They didn't emotionally explode at the child when the crime was discovered.
- They loved and advocated for their child.
- They made a police report and assisted in the investigation.
- They took their child to interviews and therapy appointments.

They led their child through a terrible experience. Their child needed and looked for a hero only to learn they live with one. In a therapy environment, this concept is called trauma-focused cognitive behavioral therapy, and the focus is on reshaping a victim's (this can be the child, stakeholder, or anyone who experienced the trauma of this event) wrong conclusions about these negative self-appraisals into something more constructive.[3] This type of therapy is commonly used with victims of sexual abuse and should be expected to be encountered in a post- victimization therapy environment.

The average human being will experience two to three critical incidents in their lifetime. Defined as a significant emotional event that breaks through a person's normal coping mechanisms and causes extreme emotional distress,[4] child exploitation fits this bill, as does the loss of a spouse or parent. But the reality is people relive the critical incident over and over again in their minds, and people tend to be extremely critical of their performance and thus spend a lot of time in an unhealthy mental state. When this author was a rookie cop working with a field training officer, and then later when he was a field training officer himself, the topic of high-speed priority response driving often came up, and there was an adage: *You'll be out of the fight if you don't make it to the call.*

In other words, get to where you need to go, but take care of yourself doing it. The greatest risk people can take is themselves. As discussed in this chapter, taboos concerning mental health have relaxed greatly in recent years, but one's own personal resistance to seeking professional help may prove to be the most challenging to navigate. No one can be entirely their own savior. In fact, in nearly all jurisdictions free or very-low-cost therapy is offered at many points in the investigative process, and it's the recommendation of this book to utilize therapy for both the child and affected stakeholders. But there are other self-care options available if a person isn't ready to acknowledge the need for therapy that are just plain healthy in general. Granted, the following list achieves best results when combined with therapy of some type.

- Prioritize quality sleep in recommended quantities.
- Eat with health in mind.
- Exercise regularly. Even a walk around the block can help.
- Take up a hobby or renew past interests that have been neglected.
- Spend quality time with family.

In other words, acknowledge the victimization and accept what cannot be changed. Realize the child victim has always watched the parent for how to be and act, and they're doing it post-victimization more than ever. Think back to chapter 14's theme: is there a plan to not explode emotionally and be that first all-important piece of the child's support network? What happens in the days, weeks, months, and even years in the household will determine how the child reacts to and deals with problems in their own family in the future.

To Recap:

- The child isn't the only victim. Stakeholders are too.
- Know the symptoms of post-traumatic stress and moral injury—trouble sleeping, lack of appetite, and difficulty concentrating are just a few.
- Take advantage of available post victimization therapies.

NOTES

1. Orth, Uli. "Secondary Victimization of Crime Victims by Criminal Proceedings." *Social Justice Research* 15, no. 4 (December 2002): 313–25. https://www.ojp.gov/ncjrs/virtual-library/abstracts/secondary-victimization-crime-victims-criminal-proceedings.

2. Williamson, Victoria, Dominic Murphy, Andrea Phelps, David Phelps, and Neil Greenberg. "Moral Injury: The Effect on Mental Health and Implications for Treatment." *Lancet Psychiatry* 8, no. 6 (2021): 453–55.

3. *Psychology Today*. "Trauma Based Cognitive Behavioral Therapy." n.d. https://www.psychologytoday.com/us/therapy-types/trauma-focused-cognitive-behavior-therapy.

4. International Association of Chiefs of Police. "Critical Incident Stress Management." n.d. www.theiacp.org/sites/default/files/all/c/CriticalIncidentStressPaper.pdf.

18

THE BACKSPACE/DELETE KEY
AND SELF-EDITING

When considering keyboard ergonomics, whether on a device or a physical one for a desktop, designers work around the three most used keys—the space bar, the "e" as it occurs in one of the most used words, "the," and the third most used key on a keyboard, the backspace key. Or for Mac and iOS users, the delete button. Because that's what humans are good at—mistakes. This key is in a very prominent position on devices.

Is it for correcting mistakes, or is it the most important self-editing tool? Composing messages and posts with the luxury of that backspace/delete key, words placed in the right or wrong order produce wholly different reactions, but most often, this key is used to show conditions in the most favorable light—a witty post, clever comeback, flirty but not too forward perhaps, cute, charming, all that good stuff. Real life doesn't have this option of course. Online interactions are carefully orchestrated, especially when the goal is the exploitation of children.

Suspects are human beings and the usual rules of attraction apply. It begins with a catch of the eye, then functions of what they're aroused by. They gauge openness and risky behaviors from the child's photos and postings, looking for curse words, likes and dislikes, drug and alcohol abuse, and especially psychological trauma and insecurities.

Very often victims' chat logs and personal interviews reveal that they've come to view the suspect as a "soulmate," the most important label to a victim. They've found somebody like them. They had the same interests in movies and music, talked about love the same way, called them a favorite term of endearment without having to tell them. In reality, all the suspect did was regurgitate what the child has already put out there, from the "describe the perfect boyfriend" quizzes to the memes posted with the hashtag "relationship goals."

The life cycle of these relationships invariably ends, and sadly, it's not because of discovery by parental authority. It's because the suspects prefer certain things about their victims. The most common characteristic is an age range, usually within a couple of years, like twelve to fifteen or nine to twelve. Next up is adolescent development, prepubescent or pubescent, followed by physical factors like height and weight. Once the child moves out of the preferred range, the suspect loses interest pretty quickly.

Or worse, the child wises up, gaining experience as the pointed questions start to come. They've wrought the damage, cut off contact, leaving the child dejected, scared, and confused. They know their self-produced pornography is in the suspect's possession and begin to wonder what's going to happen with it.

The inherent characteristic of a grooming process is a production of guilt in the victim. A bit of self-examination in one's life can find something that produced profound, deep, seemingly impenetrable guilt so it's easy to relate. Add to this an inexperienced child, and it's easy to see guilt is the key ingredient to the walls built around your child, and it'll need a jackhammer to get through.

To Recap:

- Online communications are much more manipulative than face-to-face interactions due to careful, considered responses.
- Predators take advantage of the enormous amounts of intelligence posted by the child.
- Online predatory relationships revolve around instilling a sense of guilt in the victim.

19

EDUCATE THE CHILD

The responsibility to equip children to navigate today's world of online predation runs high—especially if the child is a middle school student. Stakeholders—parents, family, guardians, and educators—all need to be tuned to this fact.

Children aged twelve to fourteen years of age are the most preyed upon online demographic.

Child predators chat among themselves as they trade images in online forums dedicated to child pornography. When investigators review these chat logs, commentaries on the physical characteristics of puberty generate huge amounts of excitement among predators. Coupled with the predator's unnatural fixation on these physical characteristics is the fact teenagers this age think about sex all the time. They're curious about it and feel awkward in their changing bodies. They're unsure of themselves, and self-esteem is in short supply.

Children this age tend to be moody and such a "joy" to be around that parents may welcome a sudden inclination the child has to spend lots of time in their room. This adds to the stakeholders' burden of guilt. As discussed, the child's not really alone anymore if that kid uses unmonitored technology.

These children are beginning to make their own decisions outside of parental control, such as whether to do homework or what clothes they're going to wear. They're aching to make their own decisions, especially when it comes to a little bit of clandestine danger. Putting one over on parents makes them feel proud. That's nothing new. Neither is the seemingly constant head-butting and unreasonable requests, such as wanting to go to the mall with their friends alone or attend an off-the-wall rap artist's concert.

The exercise of stakeholder authority creates resentment and friction in the relationship as the child pushes back against the stakeholders' goals. Add problems with best friends as they fight over boys in dramas exacerbated by text messages and social media jabs. Problems with grades and pressure to perform can leave them looking for affirmation of their looks and self-worth, and they find it in a few shiny words from a stranger disguised as an online "friend."

As the relationship progresses and the child begins to divulge problems and feelings to the predator, the suspect uses the child's vulnerability to start driving barriers between the child and their support networks.

Here are some typical comments used by online predators to drive a wedge between children and everyone else in his life:

> *Nobody gets you like I do.*
> *You're right and they're wrong.*
> *I'll take care of you.*
> *I won't put rules on you and love you enough to let you be free.*
> *Nobody will understand what we have because they're all different.*
> *You get me, and I get you, and that's all that matters.*

Phrases like this can be heady stuff to someone who doesn't yet have the life experience necessary to decipher it as complete nonsense. The result is a moody, probably rebellious teen who has a steadily eroding support network. Soon no one will want to be around that teen, and then they will be isolated. So, when a predator makes their move toward full-blown exploitation, the child will perceive that there's nobody to cry out to for help.

Victims' parents often say the worst point in their relationship wasn't the outcry or even the discovery of the crime. Instead, it was the days and weeks as the child became silent, despondent, and distant to their family while they carried the burden of a rapidly disintegrating situation.

Investigators interview the best friends of the victims too. Often, they'll report a sudden coldness or unexplained anger, followed by a cut-off of contact. Another big purpose of the wedge behavior is that it's a subtle way to reinforce what's paramount to a continued exploitive relationship: total secrecy.

What must be done is lowering the child's online flag that literally says: "Here I am, ready, willing, and unsupervised."

If there's already a good line of communication open with children about online predation, hopefully they'll bring messages from obvious online predators, including sexually explicit images, to a trusted adult. And educators, please remember some students don't have a trusted adult at home. They'll bring it to the counselor's office or during a tutoring session. The worst thing anybody can do is tell the child, "that's the way things are nowadays."

Stakeholders who chalk up exposure to pornography as a mainstream hazard of being online and do nothing about reducing that risk are producing porn-addicted kids.

PORNOGRAPHY, THE ULTIMATE GROOMING TOOL

Pornography drives more than 80 percent of all internet traffic. Arguing about whether it should stay or go is a moot point because it's not going anywhere. The internet has made pornography more mainstream than it's ever been in history. Although they still exist, the need for the old anonymous sex cinemas and the all-night XXX movie stores is almost extinct. Pornographic actors are crossing over into mainstream entertainment, a feat almost never heard of previously, with varying degrees of success. Mainstream actors are dabbling in pornography because pornography has become, well, mainstream.

Lowering standards of sexual activity shown on primetime television all but guarantees some form of gratuitous sex is available to all age members of the household. Teen boys can snicker freely at four-hour-long erections cautioned against in dysfunction commercials during football games. They snicker because they have those at that age without any medication at all. The days of temporary, intermittent exposure to pornography as developing adults are long gone. In previous generations, parents didn't have to work too hard to redirect children back toward their teachings on morality and porn consumption.

Not so now. Forensic examinations of phones have seen "blow job tips" as a search term on twelve-year-old girls' phones and "money shots" searched on boys' phones. One boy visited ten porn sites between the time his alarm went off and his mom called him down for breakfast. This mainstream acceptance of pornography has worn children's shock value down to the point if it's sent to them they wouldn't freak out at all.

Search warrants for child exploitation cases all contain what's called "boilerplate" language, standard language appearing in all warrants written. One of those paragraphs describes in detail why the scope of the warrant should include all forms of pornography and not just child pornography. It's because studies and real-life case examples have all shown that pornography of all types is used to lure children into thinking that type of behavior is what people do to each other. In the cases of physical sexual abuse, abusers will often leave pornographic materials out where children will "find" them, to arouse their curiosities and make it easier to discuss the topic.

A forensic exam on a phone found an entire six-month chat in which a thirty-year-old man exploited a thirteen-year-old boy. Very early in the conversation, the topic was pornography. The suspect sent him all manner of images, from plain vanilla sex to fetish bondage, choking, and degradation. At one point the thirteen-year-old replied, "What else you got?"

This exemplifies a stereotypical addiction, whether it's drugs or alcohol, sex, or pornography. The body and mind become inured to the amount and type of addictive substance, requiring more and more doses plus bigger doses, or in this case "bigger" shock or interest to produce the desired high. Ever-increasing amounts of bestiality and other fetishes coming into the devices as the addiction or exploitive behavior continues is common.

The idea of human sexual fetishes is pushing not just the adult pornography industry but also the child pornography underground. So if an online predator is into the self-harm fetish, *that's what they will encourage and talk a child into doing*, and use screen recording applications to record it as a permanent record.

Most adult parents would rather not find even mainstream, softcore pornography on the child's devices but can stomach finding it—which is what leads to a lenient tendency when dealing with the problem.

This can serve to allow the viewing of images to continue which will fuel an ever-increasing need for violence and degradation to get anything out of viewing pornography. A sixteen-year-old boy was arrested for possession of child pornography that wasn't appropriate for his age—he was looking at much younger subjects, as much as ten years younger than he was. The boy had become bored of the myriad of pornography he'd collected and found renewed interest in the "differentness" of toddler sexual abuse.

That's disgusting and inexcusable, but the reasoning for it can't be escaped.

To educate children, conversations with your child about pornography need to be had. Ask them what they've seen. Talk to them about the porn hits on their web history. Get them to talk about why they were looking at it. There's a good chance it'll be like anything else they've done wrong. Talking to you about it was just so uncomfortable they won't want to do it again. Because if it's not corrected, it could lead to criminal behavior.

Examples to Talk About with Children

Example One   Three fourteen-year-old boys spend the night together. In between PS5 and TikTok video surfing, one of the boys shows the others the sexting images he's collected of girls at their school. They talk about it. Maybe one of the boys doesn't like one girl for one reason or another. So they decide to make an account on Twitter, Instagram, or some other photo-sharing service for the sole purpose of "exposing" these images to their classmates and friends. The profile is made, and friend requests are sent out to those they know, along with direct messages asking them for images they have so they can be included. The profile gets a name, such as "<insert school name here> Exposed," and goes live and public. Others see the images and screen shot them, passing them among each other or keeping them for themselves. Worse, an online predator is searching for the #exposed hashtag and finds the profile, making screenshots of images which are new to him and most of the online pedophile community. Illegal trading of the images commences.

Example Two   A twenty-three-year-old recent college graduate gets his first job and soon afterward is sent on a business trip. As he's packing, he knows he'll need some computer memory to store files, so he grabs a couple of flash drives in a desk drawer and puts them in his carry-on. He leaves on a plane, conducts his business, and arrives home after a job well done, not knowing he accidentally left a flash drive on the desk in the hotel business center. A cleaning lady finds the drive and turns it in. A hotel manager plugs it in, hoping to match some documents or other indicia of ownership to a guest and return it. Instead, he finds a folder of sexually explicit images, including young teenage girls. He reports it to the local police.

The Results

In the first example, the profile gets reported and a law enforcement investigation is conducted, tracing the profile back to one of the boys' residences. In the second scenario, indicia of ownership was found, leading to the local police to contact an investigator where the young man lives. Other background information is obtained on that suspect user and the residence.

There's only so much that can be proven while an investigator sits at their desk. Eventually it's time to go out to the source and collect the physical evidence, and this is done with a search warrant of the residence. Here's where it gets a little tricky. While law enforcement may be fairly certain juvenile children are responsible for the "expose" profile, there's a chance an adult family member was responsible, acting like a child or *imitating their own child online*; it's been seen before. Also, law enforcement knows there's a chance a black sheep cousin might be living at the home, who's been arrested for a violent or otherwise heinous crime, who might not be all that happy the police are banging on the door.

Another thing about search warrant services—they're swift and to the point. If the door isn't opened in a given time frame, it's splintered by a battering ram. Entry is made by cops in all manner of bullet-resistant attire carrying long guns, turning the living room into a *Cops* episode, reminiscent of a scenario in *Call of Duty*. Doors are opened, and locked doors are kicked. People encountered are ordered to show their hands in terse voices.

People are moved toward a staging point with the rest of the collected family members. There's no time for pleasantries or modesty. Unclothed persons are afforded a blanket to cover themselves. Minor children are treated a little better because they're children, but this isn't going to prevent any bad dreams that night or the others to follow.

Dogs are barking, the neighbors' lights are coming on, and faces peek from windows. Those bold enough to come outside to ask what's going on are ordered back in their homes. Once all persons are herded, a secondary search is conducted for persons hiding in attics, in cupboards, in the garage, or in the backyard.

Investigators are asked a lot of questions which go unanswered at this point, along with, "Mister, you're in the wrong house." In the first scenario, with the teenagers and the online trafficking of their classmates' explicit photographs, a parent is interviewed and walked through the case, as they take in the information. This is where the child is determined to be the suspect or someone else is.

First, it's shock, followed by anger at both the investigator and the kid, and then acceptance as they learn their son will be charged with a crime. But the fun doesn't stop there. In order to dissuade further instances of that behavior, the investigator will identify everybody who sent images to be posted on the #exposed profile, and charge them with a crime too.

With the second scenario, the newly hired professional leaving a flash drive with child pornography in the hotel, the stakes are much higher.

In this instance, the twenty-three-year-old businessman had sexting images of girls he dated in middle and high school stored on the drive. They were in a folder marked "Hoes." He kept them for years. The girls had been underage when the photos were taken, even though they were his age then and are his age now. Granted, the folder was named and created years ago, by the date data, but the last accessed and modified dates were very recent, suggesting he managed those images, looking at pictures of fourteen- and sixteen-year-old girls, at his age of twenty-three. So, he was charged with possession of child pornography, even if it was just some ill-advised and warped trip down his memory lane.

Stakeholders have a big job ahead. The good news is that it's not an impossible job. Children have a very narrow scope of concern. Very little time is spent thinking about things more than one or two days ahead. They have blinders on. All that glitters is gold. Life experiences come along eventually and knock those blinders off. Everybody's forced to face the consequences of their actions. These days the hard knocks come earlier for children. Some knocks can be delivered by parents, and should be, in their timing and way. Translating that parental love into action to educate them about the right way to deal with online predation is the bottom line. If you don't, the predator's doing all the talking.

> **To Recap:**
>
> - While all children are potential victims, the average age of victimization is in the middle school age range.
> - Predators work hard to install a wedge between the child and the stakeholder to avoid detection.
> - There are several types of common crimes children can commit using their devices, and they need to be educated on these laws.

20

HUMAN TRAFFICKING AND SOCIAL MEDIA

A Case Study

Everyone knows a girl like Amy—bouncy blonde hair, perpetual smile, pretty with an infectious wit and the bulletproof ambition common in six-teen-year-olds. Her days are filled with the responsibilities, demands, and fun as a member of her school's drill team and Future Farmers of America, student council treasurer, and gamer club vice president.

Amy is growing up in a suburb not unlike in any other city in America, the lower end of upper class in a slightly cookie-cutter subdivision of mostly two-story homes. The streets are winding and a bit hilly with street lights harkening back to the gas lamps of old. At Christmas time, each lamp has a green wreath with a red bow at the bottom. Stay-at-home moms push strollers away from the school bus stops in the morning and afternoons, and joggers dot the sidewalks at several points in the day. Automatic sprinklers kick on in various yards with no warning to keep a seemingly impossible shade of green on the grass.

Amy's house blends right in, hers is a sprawling single-story, traditional brick with wood paneling and some stucco, painted white with black trim and shutters. The front porch is extended into the yard, with bench swings opposite each other under Edison bulb porch lights. A sign proclaiming all solicitors are not welcome, with the exception of Girl Scouts and their cookies. A wicker doormat says, "Wipe Your Paws." All of this is under the shade of a grandfatherly oak tree spared from the developer's bulldozers.

A squirrel robs the bird feeder as a cawing blackbird dive bombs from above, the comedy of which serves as an ice breaker talking with Amy's parents on that idyllic front porch on one of those last days of spring. Hints of summer are in the air. Sweat beads off the Arnold Palmer iced teas wrapped politely in a white paper napkin.

Amy's parents, Tina and David, are twenty years married as of last month. A serious miscarriage when Amy was three led them to abandon the idea of more children. Without any siblings, Amy grew close to her maternal grandmother. Their favorite activity together was going to garage sales and flea markets. But when Grandma got older and less capable, she was moved to a nursing home within a bike ride's distance of their home. Amy would often do her homework in her grandmother's room, staying to watch *Wheel of Fortune* before coming home to eat dinner.

"Tina's mother met Amy's first boyfriend, Tom, before we did," David recounted. "She ran him by her before us."

"She didn't like that boy one bit," Tina said.

For good reason, as it turned out. Tom pushed early for a more physical relationship. After the homecoming dance, Tom tried to be more physical again, and this time he became angry and dumped her. In the days following, her fellow students whispered at her as she made her way through the halls. Eventually Amy found out Tom was spreading rumors about her to salvage his fragile ego. Boys called her a prude and girls scolded her for spurning Tom, the varsity quarterback.

"That was the first major event," Tina and David agreed.

That was followed with another major blow a few weeks later in the middle of the night. Amy's grandmother passed away suddenly.

"There was an enveloping sadness around Amy, around all of us," Tina says. "My mother was older and had some trouble getting around, but she had a lot of spark left, we thought. A few days beforehand, Amy and I took her around to garage sales, which we all loved to do together."

"My mother died when I was very young, " David adds, "So I became close with her mom over the years. She was a guiding light in our lives. I could have used her crazy positivity a few weeks later when I lost my job."

David was forced to take an early retirement package insufficient for the family's financial needs. There were no more piano and guitar lessons for Amy, and the family canceled their gym memberships and other luxuries as the finances had to tighten up. David and Tina admitted they became consumed with a future they didn't anticipate. They struggled to cope, and argued more often. They almost forgot Amy's sixteenth birthday altogether.

"It wasn't a great birthday. The weekend before we sold one of our cars, leaving us as a one-car family. Amy didn't get a car like a lot of her friends did."

They did their best keeping up with Amy, but she'd taken to spending more time in her room alone. And when she wasn't doing that, she was with Tori, an old friend from middle school. Amy was zoned to a different high school, so they'd drifted apart. Tori fell in with a different crowd at the lesser affluent high school. Tori preferred dark makeup with a perpetual hoodie and ripped jeans ensemble. It was a marked difference from the fashionista Tina and David remembered her being.

"We thought we'd give her some space, as undoubtedly our home problems affected her. Our friends said that was the best thing while kids adapted to a new reality, whether it was a divorce, job loss, or the death of a loved one. We had two of those three going on," Tina says.

As David explains further, Amy's grades, once stellar enough to attract attention from a number of big-name colleges, were slipping. He and Tina would talk to her about them, and they'd improve, only to slip again. The cycle continued on and on, resulting in more and more terse discussions. Amy began to stretch her parents' patience by testing curfews, both school nights and weekends. But the biggest surprise came in the form of a phone call from the faculty advisor to the student council.

"She told us Amy was about to be replaced as treasurer," Tina says. "When we asked why, it was because she'd missed too many council sessions. One more, and she was out."

Tina and David had no idea. That night, Amy came home late, and this time reeking of marijuana smoke. They completely lost their cool. The yelling escalated at an unprecedented rate.

"Amy took her chance at the unlocked back door and ran out into the night," David says.

"It was the last time we saw her," Tina adds, dabbing her eyes with a tissue.

Amy's parents reported her as a runaway. The deputy asked if they'd tried to locate her cell phone using the data cloud functions, and they had not. When they tried, Amy's phone showed to be turned off.

"We could tell the deputy was well versed in this kind of thing. She asked for information on her social networks, email accounts, or passwords," Tina says. "The deputy was just doing her job, but it made me feel completely helpless. She didn't mean to, but her look was like 'well here's another set of parents not keeping up with their kids.' I didn't blame her. I mean, my daughter is missing and I have nothing to help find her. Nothing."

When the deputy left, her parents went through her room, top to bottom. They found weed but nothing else crazy. They asked themselves a question which would become multi-layered—What happened to Amy?

The report was forwarded to the Missing Persons Bureau. Brad Smith was the detective assigned to the case.

"I probably investigated hundreds of runaway reports during my time there. 99.9999 percent of the time it's just immature kids mad at their parents for being parents. They don't think things through very well, so after a few days of sneaking into a friend's room to spend the night, or couch surfing, they run out of places to go and return home on their own. But that doesn't mean we don't look into each and every one. It's a due diligence effort to detect any unknown problems that might escalate things. I didn't find anything out of the ordinary at first in Amy's case. An argument over bad grades and smelling like dope."

It was an assessment Tina and David agreed with when Detective Smith called them the next day.

"It didn't make us feel any better, but we understood where he was coming from. He seemed sincere in his work and, as it turned out, he'd stick with the case until he retired."

Detective Brad Smith, forty-four years old at the time Amy was reported as a runaway, had twenty years' experience in a wide swath of law enforcement duties—dispatcher, patrolman, and later as a detective with stints in auto theft, burglary, robbery/homicide, and this final stop in missing persons. There he would stay until mandatory retirement.

Six feet tall, he battles middle age and weight with regular workouts and, as he put it, a "semi-sensible diet." He doesn't fret the grays in his hair, preferring to "face the truth, no matter how ugly." Smith had a great track record with case closures, and it was for this reason he was asked to work in missing persons, with emphasis on some of the older, open cases.

"I reviewed the initial report and called David and Tina. They said she was still missing. By then she'd been a little less than a week gone. I asked about any close friends and if they'd contacted them. David and Tina said Amy had troubles at school surrounding an ex-boyfriend and had been 'taking a break' from her usual friend set. Still, they'd contacted the ex-boyfriend and a few of her friends. None of them reported having any regular contact with her in some time. They reported her to be distant, even unfriendly, but all expressed concern and said they'd call if they heard anything."

At that point, Tina and David told Brad about the phone call from the faculty advisor and the student council issue. Amy had campaigned so hard and been so proud to win that election. Again, Tina and David hadn't even noticed she stopped talking to them about the trials and tribulations of holding elected office.

"Amy recently reconnected with an old friend from middle school, Tori," Brad says. "They gave me Tori's contact information and I called her. Tori seemed surprised I was calling and looking for Amy. She said they'd talked on social media and Amy was over to her house a few times, but really didn't know her well enough again to know where she might have gone. I gave her my contact information should she hear anything."

In the meantime, Tina and David sought advice from their attorney, who put in a call to his private investigator for some tips on what they could do. There are things the police can't do quickly enough to make any kind of difference, like review bank and cell phone records without a subpoena. So they got to work, reviewing her debit card records, finding nothing out of the ordinary and nothing since she left the house. Her cell phone records were placed into a spreadsheet and sorted by the frequency of calls to the same number. Those numbers were further scrutinized by who she talked with the longest.

"The problem with that was," Brad says, "these kids today don't use the phone like we do. I mean, they use the cell phone, but not making calls using the cellular phone service. Most of these social networking apps have phone, video chat, and messaging. Amy's data usage was way higher than the actual cellular call use."

That meant Amy was a typical teenager, talking to contacts with vanity screen names like *Miguel65*, *breakerbreaker19*, and the like.

"I mean, these were all contacts in her phone, but Amy didn't put real names with those contacts," Brad says, adding that "Kids turning off their cell phones when runaways isn't uncommon, done to thwart parents' efforts to locate them via the phone or third-party applications."

Being gone five days without a peep raises more questions than answers. It does elevate concern enough to ask the cell phone provider for a certain kind of cell record—cell site data, or GPS information based upon the usage of cell towers. Everywhere a cell phone goes, it's connected to a network. In order to access that network, it needs to be connected to a cellular service tower. The last tower used just before her phone was turned off would be pretty important.

Ordinarily, it takes a search warrant to get those records outside of exigent circumstances.

"Without a warrant, it's up to the individual cell phone providers whether or not they'll give them up. Cell providers have a checklist when it comes to cops asking for an exigent circumstances disclosure outside of a search warrant. Amy's case had enough checked boxes and I got them."

The police analysis of those records provided much needed insight into what happened the night Amy left home. Based upon cell tower usage data, Amy left her residence on foot, walking to the front of her neighborhood. The speed of data connections and transfer from cell tower to cell tower revealed Amy was likely picked up in a vehicle. She traveled to the east end of town to a cluster of apartment complexes on Rogers Avenue.

"That's not a real great part of town," Smith says, "and it made me concerned."

She was likely in an apartment on the northwest portion of the Vista Grande Apartments located at 555 Rogers Avenue. The signal was live for approximately twenty more minutes before being turned off. There is not enough data to ascertain an exact apartment number.

There were no data connections since the date of her disappearance.

"This apartment complex is located on the outside edges of an area known for prostitution and drug traffic," Brad tells, "I provided Amy's photo and the report to the Vice Division with a request for a BOLO, a Be On the Lookout bulletin, to their various task forces. I went out to the apartment complex and knocked on a few doors around where the signal gave out. Nobody recognized her from the photo I had."

There's only so much that can be done with historical data from cellular connections of just Amy's phone. The location data comes from distance and angle from the cell phone towers and does provide a jumping off point to look at. In the case of personal crimes, such as kidnapping or assault, the victim's data and the suspect's data are combined and analyzed to prove both were in the same place at the same time. But in Amy's case, there was no suspect information to combine with other facts to turn into probable cause for something actionable.

The days turned into weeks. David received a call back from an interview he had before Amy left. He took a job with a local fabricating corporation in the front office. It wasn't quite the salary he had before, but added to his retirement package it erased the worries of the previous months.

Brad Smith picked up new cases, but he revisited Amy's case weekly. Things were at a standstill until he received a phone call from his agency's Crimes Against Children Unit regarding a tip forwarded to them by a social networking company.

"The tip flagged child exploitive messages. Social networks use a variety of methods to scan their site for illegal materials. The CAC (Crimes Against Children) called me because the account had been traced by IP address back to Amy's residence, which was in the system due to the runaway report. I also learned the person she'd been talking to was traced to apartment 202 of the Vista Grande Apartments at 555 Rogers Avenue, where Amy's last 'pings' to her cell phone were. Based upon this information, the Crimes Against Children unit obtained a search warrant for that apartment, and I was tasked with assisting its execution."

At approximately 5 a.m., the entry team knocked and announced on the door of apartment 202. There was no answer or movement observed within the apartment so forced entry was made. There was nobody found in the apartment, and no signs anybody had been there in some time. The apartment management said it was a furnished unit and leased to AB Corporate Housing, which is the company the internet service was under.

"With this being a blue collar apartment complex, the management said they'd seen mostly temp type workers housed there, like oilfield and manual labor types," Brad says.

The apartment complex is generally provided no information on any residents of that apartment, as the leasing entity has the keys and presumably gives them to their clients. There are no cameras in the complex except over the common areas such as the pool, mailboxes, and office areas. A canvas check of the neighbors found very little useful information, other than a handsome young adult Hispanic male and a white female, blonde, pretty, and both in their early twenties or so. They were shown a picture of Amy and none of them recognized her.

"I called Amy's parents and told them about it," Brad says.

"We were glad Brad didn't tell us about the warrant beforehand. It would have been much harder to take the news she wasn't there," Tina says.

There was one detail about the apartment Brad keyed in on, one supported by the findings of the crime scene unit. The place had been cleaned really well. No workable fingerprints—anywhere. No trash to go through for receipts. No mail. Nothing. Finally, the Human Trafficking Task Force weighed in on AB Corporate Housing. It was a known "shell" corporation suspected of association with an international trafficking organization on the radars of the Federal Bureau of Investigation, Department of Homeland Security, and Immigration and Customs Enforcement.

"At this point, the case was referred to the Task Force. It was better for Amy, as the Feds have longer arms than a local police agency," Brad sighs.

Detective Smith had lunch and coffee with Task Force members, staying in the loop and volunteering for any local assistance needed to help them. Of course, Amy's case wasn't the only one they were working on, so more often than not, Smith left his informal meetings with little new information. Almost a year later, this would change.

Amy's parents had their air conditioning ducts cleaned, and the workers found Amy's journals behind an air return vent in her closet. Clearly Amy valued privacy and did not want them discovered by anyone. Amy journaled extensively, seven notebooks of the kind available at any drug store. She favored neon colors for these diaries.

The first five books chronicled her various crushes and unreturned affections, issues with body image, favorite books, movies, and bands, drama with friends—the usual teenage problems. She wanted to get a tattoo on her eighteenth birthday and doodled many designs around unicorns and dream catchers. The last one and a half books proved to be a bounty of information on what was going on in secret, right under Tina and David's noses.

"These books were the tale of two Amys. It was just crazy, heartbreaking, and infuriating at the same time," Tina says, with David nodding assent.

The first time Amy went to Tori's house, she was surprised to find Tori on the back porch smoking marijuana with a boy and another girl. These two looked at least two or three years older; both had tattoos, and the girl had multiple piercings. All were welcoming, however, and Amy slid into the conversation about indie garage bands and underground concerts pretty easily. When the joint came around the circle to her, she hesitated at first, but eventually took a hit at their good-natured urging. The conversation turned to the marijuana, which Amy instantly took a liking to. The boy, Miguel, good-looking, dark skinned with just the right amount of musculature, knocked a few buds of the weed into a plastic bag for Amy to take home.

Then he reached into his pocket and pulled out a wad of cash secured with a rubber band, and tapped out an order for pizza on his phone. It was some pretty serious money—twenties and fifties, and it produced an aura of mysteriousness and more than a bit of bad boy syndrome in Amy.

"He's just so different," she underlined. "Confidence oozed from everywhere, way beyond any boy I've ever met. To him, it was like the world was his."

She wondered if he and the other girl, Nicole, were dating, but it didn't seem like it as the night went on. They never held hands, kissed, or looked loopy at each other. When it came time for Amy to leave for home, she exchanged social media handles with both of them, and Nicole offered to drive her.

During the ride, Nicole said she and Miguel are roommates in an apartment not far away. Although they "fooled around" every so often, they were not dating. Miguel is just a cool, laid-back guy who has money from a weed and pill operation, but other than that he's a good guy. They'd been living together since she was seventeen, and she was now nineteen.

Back at home in her room, Amy scoped Nicole's social media and quickly deduced Nicole worked as a cocktail waitress at a strip club downtown. Nicole used all the filters to make her work seem fun, glamorous even. Wads of cash, champagne on ice, diamonds and gold, and twirling human forms with "just enough blur to mask their fleshy trade."

Amy didn't remember telling Miguel anything about her grandmother or school problems, so she was surprised when Miguel asked about it online. Then again, that weed was pretty strong, to her anyways, as it was the first she'd ever smoked. Miguel was a great listener, patient and kind, albeit a little rough with an f-bomb peppered in. He said it would be okay, and he knew that because he had a rougher home life than her when he was younger and he turned out alright.

If being a drug dealer was alright, right? It was just a thing he did for money, Nicole and Tori told her. He didn't deal out of the apartment and never led customers to friends' houses just to make a deal. And besides, weed and pill users are usually pretty chill to begin with. The freaks come with coke and meth. Still, there's no way her parents would let her date such a guy.

So she'd have to sneak around to meet him, and that's what she did. At Tori's house, at the mall, and the movies. Social media calls got more frequent, and longer in duration. The topics were deeper, especially as her father's unemployment dragged on and the home tension thickened. The day before her sixteenth birthday, her parents sold the Cadillac Escalade they were still paying on, leaving them as a one-car family. There would be no car for her birthday.

Miguel taught her how to drive his Mustang, and it was a stick shift. It's only money, he said, when she ground the gears the first few times. His life was fun with a tinge of danger, and she liked being with him. Their physical relationship intensified, along with the sexual content of their messages back and forth. They started doing video calls when they couldn't meet, and they'd touch themselves for each other.

Amy borrowed the car, ostensibly to meet friends for dinner, but in reality she was picking up Nicole from work at the strip club. Her car was in the shop, and Miguel was out doing his business so he couldn't get her. Pulling into the parking lot, Amy gripped the steering wheel "like a roller coaster safety bar." She didn't want anything to do with the valets so she parked in between a shiny black BMW and a tricked out pearl white Hummer. Nicole texted Amy to drive around the back and park beside the dumpsters. Nicole held a back door open and waved for her to come inside because she was still closing her till.

The door shut behind her and Amy found herself in the dancer's green room. Girls of all shapes and sizes were in various stages of undress, doing their hair and makeup, most with earbuds in, "carrying on to their own personal soundtracks." The place was clean and smelled like berries. Amy felt like she needed a "passport to be there." Most of them were only a few years older than her. One girl shut her locker and shouldered a backpack exactly like her own, but she had a community college student ID clipped to a zipper as she strode to the back door.

Two conversed in a language Amy never heard before.

"Some are crazy," Nicole explained on the way home. "Some are single moms, others working through school." One or two were lifers, which meant they were close to thirty years old. It seemed a lifetime away, but Amy pictured "kids, an attractive, attentive husband, and a pretty house, not glitter and brass poles." Nicole tried it once, but was so nervous she threw up in a beer bucket right before her set was to start.

When Nicole was Amy's age, she made money on the internet selling her "companionship" online. There's a whole world out there in internet land who will pay money for custom-ordered pictures of an underaged girl—in certain color of nail polish, holding a cigarette between toes, high heels, and everything imaginable. Some of them paid extra for Skype sessions, just to have someone to tell about their day. There are a lot of lonely, weird people out there with money and why shouldn't a girl get her hands on some?

Amy set up a third-party payment application and Nicole let her link it to her bank account. Nicole gave her some pointers—don't use your real name or existing email accounts to set up social networks. Be careful of the backgrounds in your camera shots, don't wear a school shirt while online, stuff like that. If things got too weird, just log off. Amy would never have to do anything she didn't want to do. If the guy was nice and sweet, or was attractive, she could follow her instincts and make even more money.

With a list of fetish websites and chat rooms from Nicole, Amy waded into that world, and the money was good. One guy paid for a video of her "painting her toenails hot pink and blowing on them to dry while she said his name breathless like Marilyn Monroe sang 'Happy Birthday.'" Somebody else sent her money every time he called to talk about his day.

But then, some wanted more, just like Nicole said they would. Most of them were easy to turn down—"rude, insensitive jerks." But a few made her think twice. Nice, attractive men who kept talking about discretion, about being on the down low. The first wish she granted was to a guy who reminded her of the school principal. He wanted her to watch him masturbate.

Test driving her sexuality got her drunk on the power she realized over these men. She controlled them, and they paid her to do it. She began to see the men in her life differently, including her father, wondering if "the same wants and needs bounced around in his head." And when her parents were fighting more over the stress of unemployment, Amy began to respect him less. She felt more able to take advantage of them due to the shame of their conduct. Coming in late from curfew would have earned her a grounding not six months earlier.

One thing they wouldn't budge on were her grades, and they were slipping. The whole house was used to arguing so it just felt natural to do so with her parents. Amy spent more time with Tori and Nicole, smoking Miguel's weed. Nicole, as she handed over Amy's money from the cash application, said she left home at seventeen and never looked back. Life was so much easier on one's own terms, it seemed.

These notebooks were turned over to Detective Smith. The intelligence gleaned from them put new life back into the investigation. Analysts from the Trafficking Task Force were able to fill gaps of their own investigations, and they began to focus on Tori. To them and Detective Smith, Tori knew more than she let on initially. She was reinterviewed, and her cell phone was confiscated. From that interview and the data on her cell phone, the conclusion was Tori was a "spotter" for a human trafficking organization. A spotter is someone who gets paid a finder's fee for locating possible victims if they are successfully taken in by the organization. Tori was linked to the disappearance of two other women, along with Amy. Six other people were arrested; three of them were in another state. Tori went to jail on several felony counts related to the investigation.

Detective Smith's role in this new investigation centered around Amy's social networking data.

"At the time, there was no definitive information on Amy's whereabouts. I asked the Crimes Against Children unit for a copy of the search warrant return to the social network that made the online tip on Amy's account. The search warrant asked for all messages, emails, pictures, videos, all contents available for both Amy's and the suspect's accounts. I received a 9,391-page PDF document file. It took some time to get through."

He found Miguel's username, Miguel65, in that social media data. The account was established six months before Amy disappeared. While the account had several hundred friends and followers, it appears the operator of Miguel65 was solely concerned with Amy and Amy alone. The picture and video section contained several hundred files of Amy. These files ranged from generic selfie-style images all the way to self-produced child pornography (i.e., images which, based on the chat messages, were made by Amy at Miguel65's request). The video files ranged from Amy saying "sweet nothing"–type things to self-produced child pornographic videos of Amy.

A review of the chat messages found several characteristics of grooming-type behaviors—extreme flattery, promises of gifts and actual gifts given to Amy, attempts to isolate her from her family and friends, and, as stated previously, earnest and successful attempts to get Amy to produce pornographic material. What follows is one of these message trains, fully representative of these characteristics. This conversation took place four days before Amy disappeared.

amynwaiting—mood=zero

Miguel65—whats wrong love

amynwaiting—progress reports coming out in two days. Im in trouble

Miguel65—with parents

amynwaiting—who else lol

Miguel65—def not me

amynwaiting—I know. I wish, well, u know what I wish

Miguel65—I do, n mee too

amynwaiting—do we really have to wait until I'm 18

Miguel65—its better that way. ur parents cant do anything about it then

amynwaiting—and u won't get in 2 trouble either

Miguel65—u kno Id go through hell for u if thats wat it took but if i don't have to

amynwaiting—ikno you will if you have to I'm afraid u might once my parents get grades

amynwaiting—and they fight enough as it is. thistl give em sum thing else to focus on

amynwaiting—me. and i don't know if i can handle it

Miguel65—hmm well if it gets too bad i'll come get u and we can chill til things chill lol

Miguel65—if u gone long enough they might just be happy ur back lol

amynwaiting—for a little while they will be but then they'll remember why they mad

Miguel65—if u runaway with me be sure to pack that red thing u wore in ur pics WOW

amynwaiting—yep. toothpaste toothbrush and lingerie . . . maybe date clothes too?

Miguel65—we gotta be careful i might not want u to go back

amynwaiting—i know i won't want to

Miguel65—wanna video?

amynwaiting—in a little while parents still awake n I want to get pretty for u

Miguel65—thank god they heavy sleepers u get loud lol

amynwaiting—only 4 u gtg ttyl luv u

Miguel65—luv u

Further analysis turned up another account belonging to Amy, called amyizyours. This account was used by Amy to sell her online "companionship" in a "sugarbaby"-type arrangement. The account was consumed with text strings and pictures of a sexual nature. One suspect account, caliplaya65, paid for and received several files from Amy. This account's IP address data was identical to Miguel65's IP data, which means the traffic from both accounts originated at the apartment. The same suspect operated both accounts.

"I then took this search warrant return data to an analyst, who concluded, based upon the totality of the evidence, Amy was lured into a sex trafficking operation by the suspect operator of both accounts. The pornographic materials obtained by the suspect posing as the buyer account were likely used as blackmail to initially keep Amy compliant," says Smith.

Confirmation of this conclusion came from an unlikely source. A letter arrived, addressed to Tina and David. The letter was written by a young woman named Tiffany Sanders, who said she was sex trafficked with Amy. Tiffany seems a lot like Amy—smart, articulate, and up until several wrong turns, was headed for a bright future.

My name is Tiffany Sanders, and I was trafficked into the sex industry as a teenager. I met your daughter, Amy, when she was dumped at the stash house I was living at. She was sixteen at the time. Amy and I were forced to work at a strip club in St. Louis for several months. The traffickers kept all the money we got.

When we weren't working, Amy and I got really close. She told me she met the person who sold her at her friend Tori's house. He was older, good looking, and dangerous, and she was young and stupid. I'm familiar with that story. She had crap at school, and there were problems at home. Her grades fell off, and you and her argued a lot. She was feeling alone and helpless. Miguel, that was his name, became close and he was her first.

There was a girl, Nicole, she taught Amy how to make money selling her nudes and other stuff. She got threats from some of them. She didn't tell you because she was afraid. On the night she ran away, she was picked up by Miguel and went to his apartment. When she got out of the shower, all of her

stuff was gone—clothes, phone, backpack, everything. Miguel showed her the
pictures she sold a customer. She didn't know how he got them. He said he'd
send them all to her parents and friends. When she tried to run out, Miguel
slapped her around and locked her in a room. About an hour later, two men
showed up with guns and gave Miguel money.

They took Amy to different places, slipped drugs into her food and drinks to
get her confused and hooked. I really don't want to tell you the rest. Amy made
me promise if I ever got away and safe, that I'd let you know what I knew about
Amy, and she promised to do the same for me. She was moved out of the house I
was in while I was at work and I never saw her again. They do stuff like that to
mess with your mind, take away things and people without warning.

Amy wanted me to tell you she was sorry. She thought she knew better but
didn't. She loves you both very much, and it hurts her so much she's caused
you so much pain. I've been in a safe house for the last couple of months, go-
ing through rehab. I've been sober and good, and they allowed me to use the
internet with supervision. I saw Amy's picture on a missing person's website.
I know she's not home, and I made her a promise.

What happened isn't your fault. You were just being parents and she was
turned against you by a monster. Amy's a fighter. If I could make it, I know she
can too.

Amy's story would conclude nearly seven years after she disappeared. A UFO enthusiast was camped out in a remote desert area in southwestern New Mexico, watching and photographing the night skies. On a hike, he found the disturbed remains of a shallow gravesite. The site had been scavenged by wild animals so it was easy to deduce the human remains. New Mexico State Police worked the crime scene.

Several intact bones and fragments were collected and sent to the lab. DNA was submitted to the national database. The DNA profile was also shared with family history research companies. A hit was received from a company's data on Tina and David's DNA profiles.

They'd submitted their DNA profiles at Detective Smith's suggestion, in the event of Amy's remains being found and unidentified. He knew these companies were open to law enforcement submissions of unidentified remains in an effort to bring closure to the families of the missing.

This narrative is a "rearranged reality," a composite of actual cases in an effort to illustrate an all-too-common tragic narrative. In Amy's case, she would never return home, but it is common for these victims to be rescued or otherwise find their way back. It's from their personal accounts some universal truths can be deduced, and the reader can detect elements previously discussed, such as:

- Stakeholders in Amy's life not paying attention to her device and social media usage
- An online predator, in this case a human trafficker, using Amy's problems against her
- A patient online predator using wedge tactics to remove Amy from her friends and family

Very often these are not the result of intentional neglect on the part of stakeholders. Sometimes life events take over time which used to be devoted to overseeing these aspects of a child's life, as was Tina and David's case. A series of events like sudden job loss or the death of a loved one consumes a family, bringing everything to a complete ground stop.

In gaps caused by disruptions like this, children look for something to help them feel good again, someone to talk to who isn't consumed by a seemingly never-ending run of bad luck and misfortune. It may not even be something as devastating as what happened to Amy. It could be just the life of a typical teenager. The common thread is a systematic probing for weakness by a predator of any type, and then the inevitable exploitation of the same weakness.

Amy's first predator was Tori, and who would've imagined a teenager to knowingly lead a fellow human being toward such terrible things? The news cycle provides countless examples of tragedies befalling children who willingly left home like Amy did. Remember, if a person has enough of the right information about someone and weaponizes it, a path can be set to produce any desired result, whether it's human sex trafficking or the production of sexually explicit material.

(21)

A MONTH IN THE LIFE OF A CHILD EXPLOITATION INVESTIGATOR

To fully understand the scope and breadth of what this book is railing against, it's helpful to look at a snapshot window of a typical exploitation investigator's activities and workload for a month.

First, an investigator's work is measured by metrics like these:

- Forensic exams
- New reports
- Supplement reports
- Subpoenas issued
- Search warrants
- Public safety presentations
- Charges filed
- New cases
- Open cases

Forensic exams tabulate the number of different types of exams conducted on evidence devices and peripherals. These items range from cell phones, tablets, laptops, desktops, flash drives, SD cards, DVDs/CDs, or gaming systems. An exam would be conducted on any device capable of holding data pertinent to a case. A device could belong to a victim, a suspect, or a defendant. The exams include the use of sophisticated hardware and software to extract data and place it into a format reviewable by an investigator.

These exams vary by type of information sought, but generally these exam results display images/videos, SMS/MMS messages, chat messages from social media, emails, web histories, mapper histories, device locations, deleted artifacts, web cache, and deleted apps and their artifacts—these exams are quite extensive. The amount of time it takes to run an exam depends on the amount of data available for extractions. It's not uncommon to examine a 156 gb iPhone and find it completely full of data needing extraction.

That could be thirty thousand, forty thousand, fifty thousand, or even one hundred thousand image and video files, because the exam will capture web history cache images as well as what the device's operator used it for. There could be upward of the same amount of text messages, too. So an investigator is working not just for how long the exam takes to run. There's also the time an investigator has to take going through the data afterward for items of relevancy. Advances in this technology have greatly reduced the amount of hands-on work to sort the data, but it is still a bulky amount of time.

Remember from earlier in this book that if consent from the owner of the device is not given voluntarily, then the only other legally admissible remedy is a search warrant. So there may be time added to the process for drafting the document, receiving input from prosecutors, and traveling to the courthouse to see a judge about it.

New reports are reports drafted by the investigator. These reports could be in response to online tips, referrals from other jurisdictions, or other similar sources.

Supplement reports are smaller reports detailing follow-up efforts on existing cases. This category's totals will be much larger than the new reports, as investigators generally follow-up on reports drafted by other law enforcement personnel, such as patrolmen.

Subpoenas, depending on jurisdiction, can be written and served by the investigator or obtained directly from the courthouse.

Search warrants are more complicated. A search warrant for a residence in an exploitation case runs between thirty and forty pages long, as it not only has to include the case facts, but standard "boilerplate" language needed to satisfy Fourth Amendment and technology requirements. A search warrant for a device contains the same language but runs an average length of ten to fifteen pages. The disparity between the length of the two types of warrants is because of the type of "premise" or location being searched. Residential and business search warrants must include the results of research about occupants, business practices, and the like.

Public safety presentations can be all-day affairs if made to an entire student body, or they can be only about an hour or so in duration, and everything in between. An officer must prepare their remarks, have an outline to cover the correct material, and commute to and from the location. Keeping kids safe and their parents aware of the danger is more than worth this effort. Sometimes officers have to be scheduled to do these presentations after a full workday, if the target audience is a group of parents in the evening.

Charges filed is the goal of all the activity already mentioned. Breach of computer security (hacking), harassment, online impersonation, online solicitation of a minor, sexual performance by child, possession and/or promotion of child pornography, sexual assault of a child, unlawful transmission of visual material, and terroristic threat are examples of common charges filed by these exploitation units.

New cases are those which came in during the monthly reporting period.

Open cases are those cases currently open for investigation and ongoing work product. At the end of the month, the new cases are counted with the open cases. The purpose of dividing the two is to track the amount of incoming versus cases closed. With enough statistics in this category, trends can be analyzed as they emerge. For instance, the number of cases coming in spike in conjunction with months which include school breaks. Summer months, March (spring breaks), December, and January are the busy months in these units. The reason? Stakeholders and children spend more time together, increasing the likelihood of exploitation discovery.

Investigators can also keep daily activity reports to document how their time is spent. The daily activity report includes a section for written notes for what was done, not just where it was done, and how long was spent on the task.

In the interest of privacy and operational security, the dates as well as any subject names will be omitted. The days of the month will simply be "Day One, Day Two," and so forth. Names, locations, and other sensitive information will be marked as "*****." Any abbreviations will be explained in parenthesis. Also be aware that not every activity is noted because of time constraints.

Day One—new case intake. Child's parents received a video of their teenage daughter performing a sex act on her ex-boyfriend. Suspect is the ex, also sent derogatory messages about their daughter. Called CAC [Children's Assessment Center] *to schedule a forensic interview for a juvenile female who set up her own fetish website. Write search warrant to ***** for account contents for case *****. Intake subpoena return, review, and request subpoena for IP data based upon this return, supplement report. Write property destruction orders for recently adjudicated cases.*

Day Two—Call CPS [Child Protective Services] *in reference to a mother refusing to produce child victim for interview. Call witness for appoint-*

ment to give a statement for case ∗∗∗∗∗. Consult with DA [district attorney] for charges on possession of CP [child pornography] on ∗∗∗∗∗. DA also requested a data file copied for an existing court case. Will provide data at meeting to present case for charges. Travel to the CAC for two interviews of children relatives of recent arrestee. No outcry of abuse. Supplement results of said interviews and continue property destruction order work.

Day Three—On station at 0500 hrs for target house surveillance on search warrant for next week. Suspect observed leaving for work at 0800. Return to office, update case and search warrant document with surveillance results. Draft request for new digital camera. Called back to office on the way home to process a phone in an exigent human trafficking case. Based upon that data, assisted in after-hours search warrant drafting and execution to recover the victim and arrest two suspected pimps.

Day Four—intake suggested corrections and additions from the DA on search warrant document. 10:36–11:41, conduct forensic exam on cell phone in case ∗∗∗∗∗. Supplement case report. Intake property from evidence and supplement report after transferring evidence into new evidence location on computer. Request subpoena for case ∗∗∗∗. 11:44–3:25 p.m., conduct two forensic exams on cell phones in case ∗∗∗∗∗. While phones are processing, write search warrant for case ∗∗∗∗∗, begin review of first forensic exam, intake subpoena return from case ∗∗∗∗∗ and supplement report.

Day Five—Pick up evidence from Station 1, 10:27–2:36 p.m., conduct forensic exam on hard drive from case ∗∗∗∗∗. While that processes, intake search warrant return, review contents. Located 3.7 gb of child pornographic files from ∗∗∗∗∗. Files are of infant to toddler age range. Supplement case with file names and descriptions of representative files. Intake subpoena return from ∗∗∗∗∗ and supplement report ∗∗∗∗∗. Intake CPS case report, review, and supplement case ∗∗∗∗∗. Location checks and pictures for cases ∗∗∗∗∗ and ∗∗∗∗∗ on way home from office.

Day Six—Intake subpoena returns for cases ∗∗∗∗∗, ∗∗∗∗∗, ∗∗∗∗∗, ∗∗∗∗∗, and ∗∗∗∗∗, supplement those cases with results. Update Task Force stat report. Draft operations plan for search warrant. Travel to CAC for forensic interview, travel back, supplement results of interview and request interview disk copy.

Day Six—Draft training request, update search warrant operations plan. intake evidence in case ∗∗∗∗∗. Draft interest letters to inactive complainant in case ∗∗∗∗∗. Send final draft of search warrant to DA for approval. Finish forensic exam reviews in cases ∗∗∗∗∗, ∗∗∗∗∗, ∗∗∗∗∗, and ∗∗∗∗∗. Draft referral request for case ∗∗∗∗∗ for suspect in ∗∗∗∗∗ state. An hour before off duty, called to Station One to help in the search for a vehicle who hit a pedestrian and killed him. Vehicle and suspect were located. Assisted in drafting of a search warrant for the vehicle and tapped to interview suspect. Suspect arrested and charged. Thirteen-hour workday.

*Day Seven—Request driver's license photos for search warrant service work up. Review subpoena returns and request more subpoenas from the DA. Call parents in case ***** and explain to them their child is sexting with age-appropriate teenagers and the case will be referred back to them for discipline, close case. Draft search warrant to ***** and send to DA for review.*

*Day Eight—Review CPS case updates in cases *****, *****, and *****. Review forensic exams in cases ***** and *****, supplement findings. Travel to suspect house for interview, return and supplement findings. Suspect is likely in possession of CP based upon evasive cues. Suspect denied consent search of his home and devices. I don't have enough probable cause for search warrant of his home at this time. Give it time and be patient.*

*Day Nine—Phone rings at 2:30 a.m. for a consult call with patrol supervisor on the scene of a potentially endangered runaway call. Juvenile female dropped her phone while struggling with parents trying to restrain her. Phone is password protected, and parents don't know password. Parents suspect child is with an older male she met online. Travel to office, meet deputy at 4:00 a.m. to bypass password on phone and perform exam on phone. Discover text messages between runaway and another child indicative the child probably snuck into other child's bedroom window to sleep. Address found, deputies sent to residence, runaway recovered at 7:15 a.m. Draft administrative subpoena and court order of non-disclosure to **** so they won't alert their subscriber of the child exploitation investigation. Travel to courthouse for document review and signatures by judge, including tomorrow's planned search warrant execution. Prep for search warrant service.*

Day Ten—Wake at 3:30 a.m., get coffee, travel to office. Meet search warrant execution team, brief them on warrant service. 5:15 a.m., kit up [put on raid vests, protective gear, load needed equipment], *form caravan to search warrant location. Execute search warrant. No operators injured, suspect detained. Home is nasty. Dog and cat feces everywhere, rotting food in sink, stench is terrible. Likely human feces on bed sheets in suspect room. Fish tank with dead fish floating on top of water and live fish eating the dead ones. Suspect interview is somewhat fruitful, CP found on desktop in bedroom. Arrest made, charges filed. Contraband recovery. Back at office, tag evidence, complete arrest paperwork, draft forensic exam requests for desktop. Leave for home at 4:00 p.m., twelve-hour day for county. Have extra job until 10:00 p.m.*

Day Eleven—check out evidence from lockup from yesterday's warrant and transfer to lab. Conduct forensic exams on phones in office, find more CP on one of them. Lieutenant comes in and asks for my help on an illegal game room operation with computers likely to be found inside said game room—a typical site for child and adult sex trafficking. Come back from game room warrant, finish paperwork and supplement reports.

Day Twelve—Intake new cases *****, *****, *****, and *****, all predatory cases discovered by parents. Request their cell phones from evidence, send preservation requests and preliminary subpoena requests for affected victim and suspect social network accounts. Update case ***** and prep referral to ***** Task Force as suspect in their jurisdiction. Intake new case ***** from ***** Task Force. Suspect is in their jurisdiction arrested and possible victim in my area. Send search warrant drafts for cases ***** and ***** to DA for review. Intake reviewed search warrants, print, pending judge signatures. Review subpoena returns in cases *****, *****, and **** and supplement findings in reports.

Day Thirteen—Review case progress in case ***** then request and serve follow-up subpoenas. Review and supplement forensic exam in case ***** and *****. Intake search warrant return from *****, finding positive for CP. Case set for search warrant work-up. Make copies of requested files from the DA office for existing prosecutions. Travel to courthouse to drop requested files and get search warrants signed for social networks. Serve search warrants upon return to office. Supplement these cases. Respond to emails requesting public safety presentations. Consult with other investigators on a case. Patrol walk-in requesting dump on a phone with owner consent.

Day Fourteen—Peer review on a search warrant for a phone for a domestic violence investigator. Review of forensic exam in case ***** and supplement. Draft search warrant in case ***** and send to DA for review. Travel to courthouse to get search warrants signed in cases *****, *****, *****, and *****. Return and serve search warrants. Intake search warrant return from ***** and begin review. Positive finding of CP, case set for work up.

Day Fifteen—Prep property release of phone back to parents, meet with parents, discuss results of forensic exam. Provide advice on future device management for their daughter. Send takedown request for verified CP uploaded to *****, a porn site. Send preservation order to same site for investigation as to who uploaded said files. Meet with other investigator to peer review her case progress. Intake search warrant edits from DA, set them for signature. Send follow up emails to *****.com and *****.com for status check of subpoena processing. Call parents in several cases to give *updates on their case status and get updates, new problems if any, as they work through home issues.*

Day Sixteen—Try to recover files from a corrupted flash drive belonging to a patrol supervisor. Flash drive is imaged, and some files are recovered. Travel to °°°° school district offices to drop off subpoena for victim's student records in case °°°°°. Follow up with parents in cases °°°°°, °°°°°, °°°°°, °°°°°,°°°°°, and °°°°°. Supplement all cases with results. Complete returns on search warrants and take to court district clerk's office.

Day Seventeen—End-of-month statistical compilation and turn in to supervision. Intake subpoena and search warrant returns and supplement cases. Consult with DA on sentencing recommendations for defendant's pending guilty plea in possession of CP case. Attend guilty plea and sentencing for another defendant. Six years in state prison. Update and close cases needing closing. Property and evidence management tasks.

Day Eighteen—Best day of the month, hard drive destruction day. Collect 112 hard drives containing sexual abuse images of children and take them to destruction facility. Witness each drive going into a big machine like a much chipper shredder. It grinds them up in the loudest, most satisfying fashion imaginable. All that's left is metal confetti. These devices will never again be used to re-victimize these children over and over again. It is the final justice I can provide to victims I'll never meet but will never forget as long as I live.

The police professionals charged with these investigations are different, as this book discusses, from other investigators. Doing this job requires a mind and skill set wholly apart from their counterparts in other divisions. Even grizzled homicide detectives, who've seen terrible things people do to each other, will often remark "I could never do your job" in a conversation with a child exploitation investigator. So what sets them apart, and what can stakeholders learn from them when dealing with the fallout from their cases? In the next chapter, perhaps the biggest ally is that of faith, and it's worth taking a look at.

(22)

DO NOT SUFFER ALONE

Investigating online child exploitation crimes for any length of time brings trained professionals to a strange and disconcerting place. On one hand, tremendous differences in the lives of children are made—from preventive education to hands-on rescues of children from abuse.

But getting to those points of success has investigators enduring hundreds of hours of evidence review, frame after frame of horrendous video and image material with the soundtrack of victims' cries for help. Then there's the contrast of listening to awful victim accounts of their abuse and conducting interviews and interrogations of child abusers as they attempt to rationalize their unforgivable actions. Shell shock is a great term to describe something horrific that should never be commonplace becoming just that—a day at the office bleeding into the rest of life.

These investigations are a niche area of expertise because not many people are willing to work under these conditions. As a consequence, the cell phone rings all hours of the day and night, lending itself to being a 365/twenty-four/seven occupation. Most people can predict with reasonable certainty what a particular workday has in store for them, but this is not so for a child exploitation investigator. These unscheduled and unpredictable pulls away from being just a parent and a spouse at home when that cell phone rings, and the struggle to get back to those most important roles after that call is ended, can be difficult to accomplish. It becomes challenging to react appropriately to everyday personal life events involving trauma or tragedy—their feelings not being the first, second, fifth, or twentieth place gone to in the brain. This interruption to the ability to react and feel produces anxiety hard to bear at times.

The circumstances investigators find themselves in are not that different from the victim/stakeholder side of the equation, are they? Both are exposed to horrific abuse and encounter emotional troubles due to distancing emotions. Like investigators, stakeholders struggle with the other roles their lives require. So both sides should not wait to seek professional help. If this author could do it again, he would have set up regular appointments with a mental health professional after the first day in the office, but the better late than never adage is still applicable. After several sessions, this author was told he can move in and out of a state of emotional separation like he was changing a shirt.

However, this author didn't particularly want to be vastly separated from his emotions because that leads to difficulties down the road, and what kind of a life would be waiting when the work was over? People owe it to themselves and others to be the best version of themselves. Further therapy sessions did reveal this seemingly enhanced ability to separate more easily from emotions was an explanation as to why this author has continued to have success, and even thrive, during his assignment in a child exploitative unit for longer than the average investigator.

It's a mistake to compare one's circumstances and reaction to them to others when everyone is created so differently and for different purposes. It's also a mistake to put too much stock in a scientific explanation for how trauma is processed because it leaves little room for credit to something much more tangible, yet intangible, at the same time.

Church and organized religion has always been a part of this author's life, but to varying degrees. This author was in a Catholic school from kindergarten to fifth grade, and in middle school, high school, and college, went to church more and more sporadically. The author never finished confirmation studies in the Catholic religion and pretty much stopped practicing any form of religion in college and early adulthood. He'd still find himself praying from time to time but only when something was really needed—a good grade on a test, a job, the birth of his kids, basically all the big things.

This author slowly but surely began to deepen his faith as a result of his life—close calls at work, being surrounded by so much destruction, and a blessedly ever-long list of things to be grateful for coupled with a growing desire to understand where these blessings come from. Plus, this author and his wife wanted their children to have a strong faith foundation to help them to avoid pitfalls. After finding a church home, the children fell in with a peer set there and this faith journey continues to this day. And it was through this peer set this author got invited to a regular prayer group of men in all stages of the journey and it happened to be attended by the church pastor himself. This understanding of faith and a relationship with God deepened much faster than expected, and it led to the discovery of just how much the Bible has to say about dealing with online child exploitation.

"Therefore encourage one another and build each other up, just as in fact you are doing."

Thessalonians 5:11 explains how gossip and finger-pointing toward victims and their families as they navigate a post-victimization world is not the way to go. And it's just as important child exploitation investigators adhere to this verse with each other as it is for their peers in other areas of police work, and vice versa and all the way around.

"So do not fear, for I am with you; do not be dismayed, for I am your God. I will strengthen you and help you; I will uphold you with my righteous right hand."

In Isaiah 41:10, this author finally figured out he is not held by his own strength and that nobody really is. Human beings are designed to need and to seek Him and all that needs to be done is to simply ask, or pray, for the needed strength. It needs to be understood that adversity is an invitation to ask Him for help, because as John 16:33 says, *"In this world you will have trouble."*

There are days which still put this author's mind in a blender, but for the most part, the symptoms of post-traumatic stress this author treated early on during this type of investigative work with prescription drugs have lessened considerably. That statement is not meant to be an indictment against prescription drugs or, to a lesser extent, an indictment against secular therapy. Both have their places, and this author benefited from both and still utilizes secular therapy as part of his self-care. But, if those are a treatment, then faith is the cure in this author's experience. After this author understood the concepts of faith and not being held by his own strength alone, it became possible to move ahead without the prescription drug mood altering. As a consequence of all of it, this author leaves work most days with a feeling of satisfaction of fighting the good fight of the day rather than feeling drained with a focus on the calamities the next day always brings.

This author finally understood the Biblical principle of leaving problems at His feet. This author believes God designed him to succeed in this line of work but he also spent so much of the time ignorant of the true source of his strength. When this idea of not being held by his own strength took hold in this author's mind, the anxiety and uncertainty was replaced by a sense of almost unnerving peace. This peace is the reward for doing God's work—protecting the most vulnerable of His people. Someday it'll all come to an end, and that end will be as plain as the sun in the sky. This author won't have to wonder about it at all. God will reveal when it is time to hang it up.

Even though investigators and victims/stakeholders experience the issue of online child predation from very different perspectives, there are similarities both in how it affects each and how the devastation needs to be confronted. Faith-based counseling is hard to accept if one is not comfortable enough to accept Biblical answers. Secular counseling approaches trauma therapy in many ways but with the same goal in mind, which is to reframe trauma into an existence where it does not automatically trigger such a heavy emotional response. This author's experience with it was positive and helpful because it led to a curiosity for answers that made the acceptance of a faith-based explanation possible to finally begin to be understood. Whether the therapy is secular or faith-based, it is an imperative to healing because no one is capable of being their own savior.

To Recap:

- Seek counseling as soon as possible after experiencing a child exploitative event.
- People are always stronger than they think, and the source of that strength is deeper in more ways than one.
- Investigators and victim/stakeholders experience child exploitative crimes and care for themselves in similar ways.

23

IT'S NOT ALL BAD

The outcome of a child exploitation case has no rigid template. Each case is unique, with its own twists and turns in the path toward a resolution. Near the beginning of this book, it was mentioned that an online exploitation investigator winds up serving not only local citizenry, but those in other cities, states, even countries. If the suspect resides in another jurisdiction, as they often do, the case is zipped up and sent via secure methods to the appropriate agency.

Online predators attempt to use the cover of distance, online anonymity, and overwhelmed investigators to hide their activities. The amount of online transfers of cases from one investigator to another is crazy and constant. Sometimes the cases work out with an arrest; sometimes the investigators know in their guts the suspect did it, but try as they might, probable cause isn't proven. Other times, the suspect knows they have been compromised and destroys evidence before law enforcement can act.

Clearly, to avoid this criminal underworld is the preferable trajectory. Stakeholders doing their part to keep children safe from these online pitfalls will prepare them to take full advantage of the potential held in this tech-filled world.

Taking a walk around a college campus reveals so much energy, eagerness, and brightness on the faces of the students, and between them and the professors a palpable energy. A Tesla transfer of experience, knowledge, primers of life for those in their prime. In their hammocks, propped against trees in the quad, in the commons and cafeteria, earbuds in, screens open, fingers flurry on laptops. The same scene plays out every day, all day, in places like Trader Joe's, Whole Foods, Harvest Central, evenings at coffee houses, all night in those dorms and first apartments.

Ideas are born. Plans made. Risks taken. They're seeing value and new uses in things their parents abandoned long ago—shuttered storefronts in towns left behind by previous progress, the same progress making their times possible. They're inventing new ways and processes like apps, services, and trades to make their way in life, just like they're supposed to. These are Gen Z, and they get a bad rap with their seemingly singular focuses, "unrealistic" outlooks, and overuse of technology.

But is it overuse or preparation and practice for their shot at the world? Adults grew up with Atari 2600, Sega, and the granddaddy of the modern gaming experience, Nintendo. Most moved on into other non-gaming pursuits, but the games children are playing now were borne in the minds of gamers back then, before gamer was a word, or daresay, an occupation. What sorts of abstracts, like the threads of imagination that bore the fruit of Fortnite years ago, are forming right now in the minds of our children today? Could it possibly be Fortnite, Minecraft, and other seemingly time-wasting pursuits are actually the beginnings of teenage networking and not just opportunities for victimization, as discussed here?

As the internet shrinks the world, it brings opportunities otherwise never encountered. New jobs are made every day as these technologies are introduced. This tech revolution of the last decades is ushering in a new Renaissance. The Greeks have a word, polymath, which literally translated means "universal man." It's a person whose knowledge base is wide and deep enough to have a functional, intellectual understanding of several usable fields.

Is Elon Musk, developing cars and putting rockets into space, among other things, and other modern innovators much different than Leonardo Di Vinci, who created timeless masterpieces and envisioned things like the helicopter hundreds of years before they were possible? Since humans are the sum total of experiences, what sorts of experiences can the generations raised today come together making their futures and the futures of their kids' possible, better, and productive?

This is the reality, the permanent reliance of young people on their devices. It's their connection point. With the rising costs of college and the huge chunks of student loan debt bogging them down at key points in their careers, many are eschewing the high living costs of the big cities seeking opportunities in places they've never even been before.

Not long ago, the idea of moving to a small, dying town, making a living, and supporting a family wasn't feasible. In the age of Airbnb, a little blood, sweat, and TLC thrown at an otherwise neglected outbuilding returns it to profitability, as long as it's close to things people would want to do, and these days, people are seeking, and paying handsome sums of money, to reap that old, small-town connectivity.

What kind of a future is ahead? Only time will tell. But children today have to get there first and be ready. Ready mentally, physically, spiritually, educated, motivated, and with just enough of a bridle on their passions so they can break free when they realize their own strength. A huge part of raising them to be successful in a tech-infused environment is by melding old-school parenting and educating, timeless manners, and a knowledge and appreciation of the power handed to them in the form of a modern electronic device.

To Recap:

- Children's futures are tied to their devices.
- Children have so many more opportunities because of technology to be a productive and successful adult.
- A stakeholder's job is to do all they can to ensure children are ready and able to fully take advantage of these opportunities.

ABOUT THE AUTHOR

Jeff Lee is a career law enforcement professional with over twenty years of experience. He's a Master Texas Peace Officer with a certification in cyber-crime investigations. With a wide background in digital forensics and the conduct of criminal investigations, he also possesses a bachelor's degree in law enforcement and police sciences from Sam Houston State University. Jeff currently supervises a criminal investigations unit in Houston, Texas. He's married to his wife of over twenty years and has three sons.